The Bride Guide

The Bride Guide

THE PERFECT WEDDING PLANNER

Dinah Braun Griffin and
Marla Schram Schwartz

A Dembner Book
Barricade Books Inc., New York

Library of Congress Cataloging-in-Publication Data

Griffin, Dinah Braun.
    The bride guide : the perfect wedding planner / Dinah Braun
Griffin and Marla Schram Schwartz.
      p. cm.
    "A Dembner book."
    Includes index.
    ISBN 0-942637-39-9
    1. Wedding etiquette. I. Schwartz, Marla Schram. II. Title.
BJ2051.G75 1991
395'.22—dc20   91-18348
                                            CIP

A Dembner Book
Published by Barricade Books Inc.
61 4th Avenue, New York, NY 10003

0 9 8 7 6 5 4

To Ellen Glasgow, for her hard work and
friendship; Loretta Hess for her skillful editing;
all our friends and family for their continual
support; and most of all a very special thanks to
Larry Goss and Arnie Schwartz, for their
devotion, patience and understanding throughout
this project.

Table of Contents

Table of Contents

Introduction

I Planning Guide

The Bride Guide is a new planning concept to help you—the busy bride-to-be. Use it to organize your plans, keep track of countless details and save many hours preparing for the most exciting day of your life.

For the first time, one publication offers you a complete, up-to-date wedding planner/workbook.

Detailing everything from engagement to getaway, *The Bride Guide* includes these unique features:
• Easy-to-use worksheets to record all important planning information.
• Comprehensive articles with hundreds of suggestions to make your planning easier.
• Helpful extras such as: how to write your own ceremony, what name to choose, gift ideas, a countdown calendar and much more.

We wish you much success with your wedding and "may all thy days be as a marriage day."

Your Engagement

Your Engagement

Announcing the Good News

You've made a big decision, now you'll want to tell everyone the good news. Both your parents and his come first, of course. Even if they live out of town, they'll appreciate personal visits from you. Arrange your schedules, if possible, so you can both be there. This is the time to start planning for the families to meet soon. Chances are, the way we live these days, they've never met before. Close friends and other relatives come next. A short personal note or phone call is a way of saying they matter to you.

The pageantry and symbols of a traditional wedding are thought by some to be out of place for a couple who have shared life and toothpaste tubes for years. Those people need to rethink their attitudes.

Symbolic meanings have many layers. And, if engagement rings, bridal white or honor attendants are outmoded as metaphors for the "purity" and innocence of the bride, they are just as significant today for other reasons.

A wedding ceremony is a celebration of love, union and commitment. If it's important to you to have the old symbols represent the solemnity of the occasion, that's the only justification needed. Dismiss questions from thoughtless friends with the statement, "This is how we've decided to do it." It's not your problem if someone doesn't agree with you.

It is difficult to guess how children will react. The ones who feel more secure probably will be delighted. Others will have to be persuaded that getting a new mother or father doesn't mean losing anyone; it means gaining another person to love and depend on. Encourage the child to bring out feelings even if they're negative. A child yearns for stability above all. Your goal will be to show that the marriage will be the foundation of a strong family unit.

Tell the rest of the world through notices in your local and home town newspapers. Call the life-style editor (formerly called the society editor) to find out what's involved. Most have standard forms to fill in. Print clearly or type to avoid mistakes. And don't forget to state when you want it to appear.

At the same time, or as soon as you know the details, think about announcing your wedding. While you're at it, ask the editor for that form as well. It goes into greater detail giving, for example, occupations, schooling, parents, activities and honors. Mail it along with your other announcements immediately after the wedding.

As the baby boom generation continues to reach marriageable age, newspapers are being swamped, particularly in large cities, with engagement and wedding announcements. The solution for some newspapers has been to charge a fee for printing announcements. It's a good idea to check this first before sending yours off to the *Daily Planet*. Otherwise, it might end up in the circular file.

Large weddings usually mean you'll receive many gifts. Don't tempt a burglar by printing your home address.

The Engagement Party

The best part of wedding planning is the round of parties it triggers. Often, the first one is an engagement party. It's a great way for everyone to meet and get to know one another better. And a chance for them to congratulate you two.

Anyone may host but your parents will probably be the first to volunteer. Will it be held early in the day for breakfast, brunch, or luncheon? Or later for tea, cocktails or dinner? That's up to the host but your assistance with the guest list certainly will be welcomed.

Changing Your Mind

We all make mistakes. In the case of an engagement, it's far less painful for you and your fiancé to deal with your doubts before you say "I do" than to struggle with them after. Simply postponing the wedding date may help work out the problems. If you decide cancellation is the only answer, suffer the discomfort and start by sending a brief note to family and close friends. Phone or telegraph if time is a factor. No explanation is necessary.

As soon as possible, notify the clergymember, baker, caterer, florist, and others. Send notices to newspapers that carried your formal announcement stating:

The engagement of Ms. Rachel Stone

and Mr. Sean Smith has been broken

by mutual consent.

---

or

Mr. and Mrs. Harry Stone announce that

the marriage of their daughter, Rachel,

to Mr. Sean Smith will not take place.

If wedding invitations are already in the mail, send a printed announcement to guests using the second form above.

Return the ring(s) to your ex-fiance and all engagement and wedding gifts to the givers. Keeping busy with these activities will help you through a difficult time.

Planning Your Priorities

Planning Your Priorities

Planning Your Priorities

Striking a Balance

The '90s woman tends to be more clear-sighted about life than her grandmother. Yet, when it comes to weddings, starry eyes are still the rule. The nuptial day is romantic, exciting, memorable and complicated by the hopes and expectations of many people. You want it to be a wonderful memory, so start with the understanding that some difficult choices have to be made. And they're ideally made in consultation with, and with respect for, your loved ones.

The style of your wedding, inevitably, will be a compromise among your concerns and desires and those of your groom-to-be, the two families and close friends. But the final decision is yours and his. Don't allow yourself to be persuaded to do what makes you feel uncomfortable. Be candid about your feelings; talk over disagreements. When the great day comes, they will all be forgotten and love will conquer all.

Setting the Date

Planning is the key to a successful wedding. You can't do too much of it. A sensible starting point would be the date.

Begin by setting priorities. You and your fiancé decide which is most important to you. Is a religious ceremony important? Then it may depend on the religious calendar, or the availability of the site, or the clergymember. Have you dreamed of marrying in the mountains or with the roaring surf as background music? We all have a dream of the perfect setting. Does an urgent business commitment take precedence? Decide which will be your pivotal point and set your date according to it.

Juggling countless details will become easier with practice and a well-organized plan.

Budget Decisions

It's difficult to consider very practical matters like money when you really want to throw all caution to the winds and have the wedding of the century. You must consider your budget. Everything else hinges on it.

Today's economy makes even the simplest celebration costly. Traditionally, the bride's parents paid for the wedding. But this can be a heavy burden and the rules are bending. It's best to discuss the subject candidly with both families to work out the best solution for everyone.

Your groom's family will be able to decide more wisely — on their guest list, for example — when they know what the limitations are. Encourage open discussion about money matters, particularly when his family offers to share expenses. You'll avoid disharmony and they'll feel more involved.

Any division of expenses that makes everyone happy is acceptable. Nowadays, financially capable couples often pay for their own wedding. As a starting point, the following page lists the traditional division of costs. But first, here are some suggestions for controlling expenses:

• Take advantage of pleasant weather — have an outdoor barbecue party after a summer wedding.

• Ask friends or family to prepare the wedding feast.

• Serve simple, inexpensive food with beer and soft drinks.

• Make or borrow a bridal dress, hat, or veil.

• Serve champagne punch instead of champagne.

• Use a soloist, trio, or sound system with disc jockey, instead of an orchestra.

• Hold the rehearsal party at home and serve sandwiches.

• Order your and/or the bridesmaids' dresses from a discount department store catalog. These prices can be very reasonable, but make sure you order early.

• Hand make gifts for attendants.

• Plan your honeymoon to coincide with off-season prices.

• Plan an afternoon reception and serve light food and wine punch.

• Ask your professional caterer, florist, and other wedding specialists for money-saving suggestions.

Who Pays for What

You and/or Your Family

• Invitations and announcements

• Engagement party

• Flowers for ceremony and reception

• Musicians and/or entertainment

• Groom's gift

• Groom's wedding ring

• Gifts for bride's attendants

• Attendants' party

• Your medical exam including blood test

• Thank-you notes

• Wedding gift book

• Wedding guest book

• Wedding dress, veil, accessories and trousseau

• Rental fee for ceremony site and gratuities

• Rental of aisle carpet, ribbons, canopy, tent or other accessories

• All photography

• Lodging for bridesmaids

• Transportation for wedding party

• All reception expenses

• Rehearsal party

• Bridal consultant's fee

• Valet parking services

Groom and/or His Family

• Engagement and wedding rings

• His medical exam including blood test

• Marriage license

• Officiant's fee

• Gifts for groom's attendants

• Flowers for you, your bridal party, mothers, grandmothers and honored guests

• Boutonnieres for groom's attendants

• His wedding attire

• Your wedding gift

• Lodging for out-of-town ushers

• Honeymoon

Attendants

• Travel expenses

• Wedding attire

• Parties or entertainment for the bridal couple

Wedding Expense Record

	Amount Billed	Deposit Paid	Balance Due	Expense of Bride/Family	Expense of Groom/Family
Stationery					
Engagement Party					
Rehearsal Party					
Consultant/Coordinator					
Ceremony					
Officiant					
Women's Wedding Attire					
Men's Wedding Attire					
Bakery					
Caterer					
Flowers					
Photography					
Musicians/Entertainment					
Reception					
Transportation					
Special Services					
Misc.					
Total					

Notes

The Officiant

This person can be an invaluable planning resource; schedule this appointment among the first. He or she will explain the details of traditional ceremonies and help you plan an untraditional one. In the case of a religious ceremony, the clergymember will know about prohibited days. It's especially important to discuss religious aspects when the bride and groom are of different faiths. Also, since many interfaith marriages nowadays are performed by clergy from both denominations, you may have to make double arrangements. Be sure to mention it if you plan a double ring ceremony.

You'll want the rehearsal to be at the wedding site, if possible. This means defining the date, time and availability of the officiant well in advance.

Ask about rules and regulations for photographs, decorations and candlelight ceremonies; special equipment such as canopies, aisle carpets, extra chairs, candles, wine glasses and kneeling cushions; and live or recorded music unless you're making your own arrangements.

More than a few wedding planners weigh the setting's beauty, and the size — will guests overflow an intimate chapel or look lost in a cathedral's immensity? Or, when the reception is being held there, are the facilities adequate? In any event, investigate practical matters: sufficient parking space, secure dressing rooms with good lighting and mirrors, for example.

Ask about the fee as well. Judges and justices of the peace routinely request a flat fee. Clergymembers' fees, however, vary widely and are based on your income, the time involved, and the size and appointments of the ceremony. Some fees cover everything, others include only the use of the facility with additional charges for wedding director, candles, organist, custodial and other services. Be sure you know exactly what's included before you make your final choice.

Setting Your Style

Basic Wedding Styles

Most bridal couples today set their own style, combining a little of the old, something of the new with a large dash of imagination. But, to begin with, there are four traditional basic styles, each one dictating what you do and how you do it. How you combine them — or discard them — is up to you and depends on many factors of custom, budget and personal preference.

Very Formal

Usually held in a church, synagogue, temple or hotel. It includes engraved stationery, formal portraits, and a large reception dinner, seated or buffet, with many floral displays, an orchestra and a limousine standing by. There are between four and 12 attendants: one usher for every 50 guests, maid and/or matron of honor, best man, bridesmaids, a flower girl or two and a ringbearer. Very formal weddings are usually arranged by a bridal consultant and the costs are very high.

Formal

Generally this means the same elements as very formal but on a less elaborate level. It may be held in a religious setting, hotel, restaurant, banquet room, private club, or in a home. Engraved invitations are still the rule with separate reception cards. The reception is large and arranged by a bridal consultant or the bride's mother. Four to 12 attendants and one usher for every 50 guests is common practice.

Semi-formal

Offers more opportunity for variation than formal weddings. Location choices may be the same although ceremony and reception are often held in the same place. A single engraved invitation for both will do, or it may be handwritten. Choice of wedding attire and flowers, for instance, is more individual. Simple decorations may be done by friends or family, and formalities like an aisle carpet eliminated. Usually attendants number two to six with the same usher/guest ratio.

Informal

No rules aside from those of dignity and good taste. Often it is a daytime ceremony, in street dress, with a few relatives and friends. Handwritten or telephone invitations are appropriate. The setting may be a home or some other informal location, outdoors perhaps. Flowers and decorations are optional.

Variations

Rectory or Chapel Setting

Requires only parents and two legal witnesses present. The ceremony is very informal although prior arrangements must be made with clergymember.

Civil Ceremony

Usually performed in judge's chambers or registrar's office, but may be held at home or in a hotel or club. Two legal witnesses are necessary. Guests and attire are optional.

Double Ceremony

Significantly lower costs — a major advantage. One follows the other using the same attendants, if desired, and equipment. Use harmonizing color schemes and styles for individual distinction. Any question of precedence can be decided by age. Balanced against the money-saving advantage is the need to share the spotlight on a very special day.

Military Wedding

Usually formal and demands a certain protocol. Some officers must be invited and assigned seats of honor, for instance. It's best to verify the rules with the proper authorities. Times are changing and today the military officer may be the *bride*. Either sex may be married in uniform but only men carry sword and saber. Because weapons are worn on the left, the bride stands on the right. Military men never wear boutonnieres.

Decorations are usually red, white and blue with American flags predominating. Military guests are seated at the reception in order of rank. The bride and groom, by tradition, cut the wedding cake with a sword or saber.

Religious Ceremony Practices

We have a culturally diverse country. Yet our marriage ceremonies are similar in many respects, though some denominations have distinctive features. Wedding attire and the order of events generally are the same. But clergymembers have individual preferences, and you'll be adding special touches, so discuss these points as soon as possible. If you're not a member of the congregation where you're marrying, know their practices to be sure they correspond with your beliefs. Here are the wedding practices of the major religions:

Protestant Ceremonies

Most churches follow a standard marriage ritual. Clergymembers are reluctant to perform marriages on Sunday or holy days although no laws prohibit it. Music rules vary: some churches permit secular music, others don't. It's sensible to get approval before making final arrangements. Many wedding gowns come with jackets or capes because modest attire is generally preferred by the clergy.

When the minister asks, "Who giveth this woman to be married to this man?," the bride's father steps forward, takes her hand and gives it to the minister or groom. Many fathers follow the charming custom of kissing the bride before taking a seat. Before beginning the familiar "dearly beloved" service, the minister ascends the altar steps. Bride and groom then ascend, followed by honor attendants who stand below them and to the side, and finally other attendants stand behind them in pairs. Marriage vows end with "till death do us part." Guests stand during the processional and parts of the ceremony according to the minister's instructions. Many couples end the ceremony with the Lord's Prayer.

Other major Protestant denominations follow these variations:

Episcopal: Formal weddings are discouraged during Lent. At least one partner must be baptized and pre-marriage counseling is often required. Divorced persons may remarry though sometimes dispensation is necessary. If both bride and groom are congregants, a nuptial Mass, or Eucharist, may be celebrated and Communion distributed as part of a "high" Episcopal service. The marriage ritual begins with a betrothal ceremony after which the father gives away the bride.

Mormon: The Church of Latter Day Saints recognizes two kinds of marriage ceremonies. The first, restricted to those who meet certain requirements, is held in a Mormon Temple. These vows declare the couple to be wed "for time and eternity." The second is a civil ceremony performed by a bishop or civil official. Interfaith marriages must use the civil ceremony. Mormon couples may remarry in the temple when they meet the requirements.

Quaker: Congregations must approve a couple's intention to marry, a process which may take up to three months. The Society of Friends believes only God can sanctify a union; no one gives away the bride or pronounces the couple married. In the usual practice, the bridal couple enters a regular meeting together and joins the seated congregation. They all meditate until the bride and groom rise, join hands and say their vows. A member of the meeting brings the marriage certificate for the couple's signatures and reads it aloud to the congregation, after which everyone present signs it. Some Quakers have bridal parties, rings, music and floral decorations. But the typical ceremony is quiet and simple in keeping with Quaker tradition.

Eastern Orthodox Ceremonies

Eastern Rites churches, including the Greek and Russian Orthodox, follow the Catholic tradition in many ways but don't recognize the authority of the Pope. Interfaith marriages are allowed if both are baptized Christians. A religious decree of annulment and a civil divorce are required for remarriage. Many Orthodox denominations publish marriage banns, and forbid weddings during a season of fast or on certain holy days.

The Orthodox ceremony is long and rich with symbolism. It begins with a betrothal ceremony blessing the rings which the bride and groom exchange three times and wear on their right hands.

(Many of the rituals are repeated three times, signifying the Holy Trinity.) The couple wear crowns, or have them held over their heads. After the Gospel is read, they share a cup of wine symbolizing the joys and sorrows they will share. The ceremony closes with the congregation singing "God Grant Them Many Years."

Jewish Ceremonies

Judaism is divided into three groups: Orthodox, Conservative and Reform. No single set of wedding practices is followed by all three. Rabbis differ in their interpretations too. Many will not marry an interfaith couple. Orthodox and Conservative rabbis recognize only religious divorce decrees; Reform rabbis accept civil divorces.

Jewish weddings can take place in a non-spiritual setting though the trend is back to a synagogue or temple. Most are held on Saturday after sundown or on Sunday, but they may be held any day but the Sabbath, during Passover and certain other holy days. Wedding attire is conventional except that, for Orthodox and Conservative ceremonies, all men wear hats or *yarmulkes* (skull caps) which are usually provided for guests.

In Jewish ceremonies, the rites are performed under a *chuppah,* or heavily ornamented canopy, signifying a tent in nomadic times and a home today. Some of the ceremony is in Hebrew. It ends with the traditional seven blessings. The bride and groom sip blessed wine from a glass and the groom crushes it underfoot. Everyone present wishes the couple *"mazel tov,"* or good luck.

Roman Catholic Ceremonies

Marriage banns must be announced three times — during Masses on Sundays or holy days, or in the church calendar or bulletin. For an interfaith marriage, no banns are published. The non-Catholic must be free to marry; that is, the Catholic must obtain dispensation from the bishop of the diocese. Divorced Catholics may not remarry without a church-sanctioned annulment.

Priests usually require pre-marriage counseling to discuss the obligations and pitfalls of marriage. Catholic brides need permission from their pastors to marry in another parish. Nowadays,

priests will co-officiate with a Protestant minister at an interfaith marriage.

Ceremonies are similar to Protestant ones in most respects, except that the father does not give away the bride. Some pastors will not approve of secular music. Weddings are held during Lent and Advent but decorations and style may be more subdued. Catholics marry at a Nuptial Mass, with Communion, before noon, or in an afternoon ceremony. Mass books are usually provided for guests although non-Catholics are not expected to join in the responses.

Writing Your Own Ceremony

*M*any couples are composing their own ceremonies, borrowing from different traditions and adding creative touches of their own. It's the most personal way you can express your deep feelings about the promises you're making.

Consult with your officiant first; the best source of ideas is the expert. Ask for books on traditional and alternate services and design the ceremony that's right for you. If you're worried about stage fright, have him or her read the vows you've written.

Check with a librarian, too. Literature and poetry are rich sources of inspiration. Be sure you develop a logical presentation whether you borrow the words of another or use you own. As an example, start with your feelings about the nature of marriage, speak of your commitment and depth of your love, followed by your sense of mutual obligation — an ideal place to mention the children in a second marriage. Compose the vows from the depth of your emotions and you'll find the right words.

Add symbolic gestures to your loving words. Each of you hands a single rose to your new mother-in-law, or have a friend or relative present a rose to each arriving guest. Have members of the bridal party or important guests read from the scriptures to symbolize your community. Or ask everyone to end the ceremony with a handclasp of peace.

Origins of Traditions

Like holiday traditions, bridal customs are a blend of many cultures and eras. Some origins are so obscure they have no relevance to modern marriage. Yet, more than at any other time, weddings bring out a yearning for the traditional. And we use the old customs to celebrate the continuity of life and family.

- *Rings* date back to a time when cavemen tied braided grass circlets around the bride's wrists and ankles to keep her spirit from escaping. Later, rings were made of leather, carved stone and crude metal.

- *Diamond engagement rings* first appeared in medieval Italy when precious stones were considered partial "payment" for the bride and a symbol of the groom's good intentions.

- Engagement rings are worn on the *third finger, left hand* because the ancients believed its vein led directly to the heart.

- The *best man and ushers* were originally burly friends who helped capture the bride-to-be. Suitors often had to fend off overprotective brothers or other suitors. It made sense to bring along the best men for the job.

- The *maid of honor and bridesmaids* protected the bride from an overprotective brother because she wanted to be kidnapped. When the rough practice became unfashionable, the pretense continued to add excitement. Besides, to go willingly was considered unmaidenly.

- The *veil* began as a sign of modesty. Some cultures, particularly in Asia and the Middle East, still follow the custom of hiding the bride's face until after the ceremony. The custom continues in our open society because of its romantic aura.

- Nelly Curtis, it's said, started the fashion for *lace veils* when she married President Washington's aide. Her fiance was so taken with her beauty after seeing her through a curtain, Nelly added one to her bridal costume.

- Rowdy 14th century wedding guests in France scrambled to remove the bride's garter believing it brought them luck. Embarrassed brides began removing it themselves (and later their stockings) to toss to the eager crowd. Eventually, this custom evolved into the more dignified *bridal bouquet toss* to foretell who the next bride would be.

- The *bridal shower* originated in Holland. The legend says a Dutch father opposed his daughter's marriage to a poor miller and refused her dowry. Her friends "showered" her with gifts to help her set up housekeeping.

- *Giving away the bride* dates from the days when daughters were chattel. Nowadays, fathers (and mothers) walk down the aisle with their daughters to show pride and approval.

- *Trousseau* comes from the French word for bundle. Originally, the bride brought clothes and household articles wrapped in a bundle. This humble container became inadequate as the dowry expanded to add to the bride's value in the eyes of her suitor.

- The *wedding cake* began in ancient Rome. A thin loaf of wheat bread was broken over the bride's head to insure a life of plenty. The guests eagerly ate the crumbs as good luck tokens. By the Middle Ages, English brides and grooms kissed over a mound of small cakes. An enterprising baker put the cakes together, covered them with frosting, and the modern tiered wedding cake was born.

- *Throwing rice* started in the Orient as a wish for many children.

- *Old shoes* used to be thrown at the bride by her father to signify he was giving her to the groom. The shoe was a symbol of possession and authority in the good old barefoot days. Another version says they were thrown at the groom as he kidnapped his bride.

- The bride was *carried across the threshold* because she was reluctant. At least, in Roman times, she was supposed to be reluctant. Or, another story says, evil spirits haunted the threshold and the bride was carried over it to protect her.

• The *honeymoon* originated with the ancient Teutons. Couples married under a full moon and drank honey wine for thirty days.

Cultural Customs

Every culture has its own charming wedding customs. Use your imagination and adapt one from the land of your ancestors. We've researched a few and a librarian will help you probe further.

Africa
"Mayst thou bear 12 children with him" is still the common salutation to brides in remote areas. Many tribes marry the couple by binding their wrists with plaited grass.

Afro-American
On antebellum plantations, brides believed Tuesday and Wednesday weddings guaranteed them a good husband, long lives and happy days.

Bermuda
Newlyweds plant a small tree in their garden. As it grows and strengthens, it symbolizes their love.

Belgium
Brides carry a handkerchief embroidered with their name. After the ceremony, it's framed and displayed until the next family bride adds her name.

China
Two goblets of honey and wine are joined with a red ribbon — the centuries-old color of love and joy — and the couple exchange a drink of unity.

Czechoslovakia
Brides wear wreaths of rosemary for wisdom, love and loyalty.

England
A country bride and her wedding party walk to church on a carpet of blossoms to assure a happy path through life.

Finland
A bride once wore a golden crown during the ceremony. Later she was blindfolded while un-married women danced around her. Whoever she crowned was predicted to be the next bride.

France
The bride and groom drink a reception toast from an engraved silver two-handled cup, called a "coupe de marriage," and pass it on to future generations.

Greece
Couples hold candles decorated with ribbons and flowers.

Holland
A bride and groom sit on thrones under an evergreen canopy — for everlasting love — during a pre-wedding party given by the family. One by one guests approach and offer good wishes.

India
The groom's brother sprinkles flower petals on the couple at conclusion of ceremony. Each family has prepared puffed rice which is mixed during the ceremony for prosperity and fertility.

Iran
In Persian times, the groom bought ten yards of white sheeting to wrap around the bride as a wedding dress.

Ireland
December 31 is considered the luckiest day for weddings in the Ould Sod.

Italy
Since Roman times, couples have walked through the village passing out cakes and sweets.

Japan
The bride and groom take nine sips of sake, becoming husband and wife after the first sip.

Cultural Customs

CONTINUED

Jewish

For centuries, couples have had a marriage contract in the form of written vows, called a *ketubbah,* which is embellished by an artisan with bible verses and decorative borders symbolizing the home.

Lithuania

Parents of the couple serve them symbols of married life: wine for joy, salt for tears and bread for work.

Mexico

A white silk chord is draped around the couple's shoulders to indicate their union. Later, guests hold hands in a heart-shaped circle while the newlyweds dance in the center.

Philippines

The white silk chord custom is practiced here as well as Mexico. All wedding expenses are met by the groom's family, who give the bride old coins symbolizing prosperity. The bride's family presents newlyweds with a cash dowry.

Poland

Brides wear embroidered white aprons over their gowns. Guests discreetly tuck money into its pockets.

Rumania

Wedding guests toss sweets and nuts at the couple to wish them prosperity.

Russia

Wedding guests, other than family, receive gifts rather than give them.

Spain

Brides wear mantillas and orange blossoms in their hair. Grooms wear a tucked shirt hand-embroidered by the bride.

Sweden

Brides carry fragrant herb bouquets to frighten away trolls and grooms have thyme sewn into their wedding suits.

Switzerland

Junior bridesmaids lead the procession tossing colored handkerchiefs to the guests. Whoever catches one contributes money for the couple's nestegg.

U.S.A.

Early Americans gave the honeymooners sack posset, a hot spiced milk and brew drink, to keep up their energy.

Wales

Brides give attendants cuttings of aromatic myrtle. When one blooms, it foretells another wedding.

Start a New Tradition

• In Jewish ceremonies, the traditional *chuppah,* or canopy, is made of velvet or other silk material and decorated with fringe or embroidery. Make yours of fresh flowers and fragrant greens instead.

• Non-Jews might adapt this lovely custom by using a canopy as a striking decoration or to designate an altar in a non-church setting. Design your own, and perhaps make it by hand, with symbols, fabrics or decorations that have special meaning for you.

• Candles set the mood at many weddings and receptions. Some florists, rental agencies and churches rent small candleholders for the ends of pews and large floor stands to hold tall candles. Add to the glow by writing a candlelight ceremony during which you light a handheld candle from a large altar candle when you speak the vows. Or line a pathway during an outdoor evening service with small paper bags, half-filled with sand, holding a candle each.

• Float helium-filled balloons against the ceiling of your reception room. Then guarantee a rousing party finish by asking your friends to dispose of them before they leave. They won't be able to resist popping them.

• Ask your bridesmaids to burn incense in the choir loft to give the ceremony an exotic flavor.

Setting Your Style

• A bride whose family emigrated from the Middle East years ago stood with her groom on the antique oriental rug they will one day inherit. Is there a family heirloom you might use?

• Decorate a home wedding with yards and yards of wide ribbon ornamented, at intervals, with clusters of flowers.

Choosing the Setting

Years ago, before mobility became our way of life, weddings were often held at the same location generation after generation. That's hardly ever true nowadays, of course. But if you're wistful about the passing of some traditions, the good news is that today you're free to express your individuality by choosing the ceremony and reception settings that suit you.

Without question, combining them in one place is the most convenient. It minimizes traffic hassles and saves time — often money. Some religious facilities and many commercial establishments are equipped to serve the double purpose. How you mix them, or match them, depends on your personal style, budget and possibly religious affiliation.

Religious Facilities

Some devout couples make all the wedding plans at their place of worship because it is the center of their lives. Others hold a reception at the same place their marriage is blessed because of convenience. Consider your priorities and whether any building restrictions or behavior codes fit in with your party plans.

Hotels, Banquet Rooms and Reception Halls

These settings are popular because of their flexibility and comprehensive services. Turn all your worries over to them. Or give them the responsibility for some matters and coordinate the rest yourself. Some have package deals which can include a chapel and every detail from invitations to food and music. Use the wedding director as an expert source of advice once you've made your choice. You'll find a detailed guide in the Service Guide Section of the *Bride Guide*. Study it and

perhaps make up a checklist of questions before you begin the survey.

Rental Hall

The most basic halls are merely space for rent, with kitchen facilities generally available. Local fraternal and service groups often rent halls to meet the expenses of maintaining their own center. Otherwise, halls vary in size, equipment and the services they offer from catering a seated dinner for six to auditoriums complete with stage and public address system. Begin by knowing your budget and what services you'll coordinate yourself. Ask for a tour of the facilities and an estimate of the costs. Very low cost is sometimes deceiving. It may mean you have to pay tor extras — and almost everything is extra. The great advantage of rental halls is economy. Formal weddings are seldom held in this type of setting.

Private Club

A private club has some of the advantages of a home. It's familiar, usually secluded, exclusive and the staff is like family. Few private clubs open their facilities to nonmembers. But if you're lucky enough to have a close friend or relative with a membership, you might ask that person to host your wedding. Try asking the chamber of commerce, or business association, in your area if any local private clubs welcome nonmembers for special parties.

Casual Home or Garden

There's a special warmth about a home wedding that's hard to duplicate anywhere else. Familiar faces in familiar surroundings are so reassuring. It can be professionally run by a bridal consultant, caterer and all the other experts. Or you can rally your own troops for a do-it-yourself wedding.

The work doesn't have to be overwhelming. In fact, the secret is to plan every detail in advance and enlist everyone's cooperation. Be sensible, make your plans simple and workable. You'll find that weddings, like all festive occasions, take on a life of their own. Once you've started the ball rolling, you can relax and go with the flow.

Plan areas, indoors and out, for the ceremony and receiving line and for separate food, beverage,

Choosing the Setting

CONTINUED

dancing and conversational centers. The secret to a good party is movement. Place a buffet, for instance, where the natural flow will go from it to a casual eating area. Or use small tables scattered about but be sure and designate the head table ahead of time.

Make up your own worksheet including everything down to the ashtrays in the smoking area. Give everyone a specific responsibility. If you're cooking and serving yourself, plan simple foods that won't spoil in the heat and serve buffet. Experiment ahead of time till you find just the right delicious recipes. Caterers or rental dealers will supply you matching china, glassware, flatware and linens for a large crowd. The morning of the wedding prepare simple sandwiches or canapes for a cocktail reception. Or make them well in advance and freeze.

If you're having under 30 guests, consider serving a luncheon or dinner at small tables. Have a separate table in an attention-getting spot for the wedding cake. Order from a bakery or do it yourself with fancy icing decorations or fresh daisy chains or ribbons.

Serve bubbly champagne, still wine, or an exotic fruit punch, spiked or nonalcoholic. The professionals say to figure two four-ounce cups of punch per hour per guest and you'll have enough. Add a safety margin to that if it'll make you feel more at ease. And have several batches made in advance so your ''punch manager'' can replenish the bowl easily.

Everybody loves a party. You'll have the best time of all at your own reception if you plan carefully; serve well-chosen, tasty food and drink in generous amounts; keep the expenses within your budget, and do as much as possible in advance.
Beautify the scene with a professional florist's touch, use blooms from your own garden, or decorate with bells, candles or balloons. (One caution with candles — place them out of very hot sunlight or strong drafts.) Finally, have a musical background and, whether it's formal or informal, your home wedding will have a special flavor.

Formal Garden

The warm summer months are perfect for a garden wedding. Even so, don't leave anything to chance — have a second indoor setting planned just in case the unthinkable happens. The outdoor ceremony site should be placed by a lovely focal point such as a trellis in bloom, a sparkling fountain, or a stately old tree. Try to position it so that the sun will not shine in guests' eyes. If the garden has a particularly striking floral color scheme, coordinate your bridal party attire with it. Food and beverages are usually served under a tent or marquee for this formal affair. Music is not essential but a musician strolling among the guests is a nice touch. Remember, however, that something, perhaps a recording, must catch everyone's attention for the processional when you want all eyes focused on you.

Grass stains are the devil to remove; spread an aisle canvas to protect your train and leave orders no lawn watering is to be done the night before. Formal garden weddings are usually professionally done and coordinated by a bridal consultant.

Ships/Boats

The smell of the sea and cool ocean breezes are irresistible to anyone but a confirmed inlander. Shipboard weddings are unconventional but great fun. Use a nautical theme for decorations, clothing, even food. Larger ships provide equipment, tables and chairs, beverages and food. Or rent a smaller vessel, bring along the crew and a picnic and start married life watching a magnificent sun setting slowly in the west.

Mountains/Beaches

The great outdoors is a spiritual cathedral, no setting could be more romantic or picturesque. Choose the natural terrain where you met or where you spent many happy hours, dress casually, bring along wine, cheese, fruit and your close friends. Have a clambake at the beach or rent horses. Worried about rain? Pick someplace with a shelter nearby. Don't forget insect repellent and spray to keep out unwanted 'guests.' Professional exterminators will spray an area that is close to the city. Use a tent for fancier food, where the terrain is flat, and tables and chairs if you want to be very, very

formal. The beauties of nature will be your decor. Ask a friend to bring along a guitar. Or hire professionals with nonelectric (acoustical) instruments. There are many possibilities for outdoor weddings. If you don't have a personal favorite, call your city, state, or federal parks department for ideas, or the local visitors and convention bureau.

Museums

Many museums, historic places, arboretums and formal public gardens encourage weddings. Sculpture gardens in the East and Spanish mission churches in the West have been the scene of beautiful weddings blending the old with the new.

Public or Historical Sites

There are many beautiful old mansions that over the years have been donated to cities and are open to the public for tours. Many of these buildings can be rented upon request. The cost varies so check their fees and availability. You might also want to check out the numerous museums, arboretums and formal gardens highlighted in your local newspapers and phone books. The Chamber of Commerce is also a good source of ideas for wedding sites.

Types of Receptions

Once you have determined where your wedding/reception is to be held, along with what your budget, style and time will be, then you can concentrate on the type of reception you desire.

MORNING — A breakfast or brunch reception is nice following a morning wedding at 9 or 10 A.M. This may be served buffet style or guests may be seated at specified tables. Egg omelettes, fresh fruit, croissants, rolls, and quiches with a variety of cold cuts and cheeses are nice. Pastries or a wedding cake can be served as well. Champagne, wine, or mixed drinks are optional, but hot coffee and tea are a must.

LUNCHEON — These are similar to brunch receptions and may be either sit-down or buffet style. They generally follow a late morning or high noon ceremony and are served between 12 and 2 P.M. They may include a variety of salads, sandwiches and cheeses. Your reception coordinator or caterer will have suggestions tailored to your budget.

TEA OR COCKTAIL — Tea receptions are generally held between 2:00 and 5:00 P.M. Coffee, tea or punch are generally served with or without champagne or wine. Tea sandwiches or other finger food along with wedding cake are usually offered. This type of reception is the least expensive to have and therefore can be perfect when there is a large guest list and a small budget. Cocktail receptions are held between 4:00 and 7:30 P.M. Usually champagne, wine, punch, or beer are served and depending on the budget, there can be an open bar. Hot and cold hors d'oeuvres can be passed around or set out on tables.

Ceremony Estimate Worksheet

	Estimate No. 1 Name ___ Phone ___		Estimate No. 2 Name ___ Phone ___		Estimate No. 3 Name ___ Phone ___	
	Description	**Cost**	**Description**	**Cost**	**Description**	**Cost**
Site Rental (if any)						
Officiant						
Services: Cantor, Sexton, Altar Boys, etc.						
Equipment: Cushions, Kneelers, Altars, etc.						
Misc.						
Total						

Officiant Choice:

Name ___

Address ___

City ___ Phone ___

Ceremony Choice:

Name ___

Address ___

City ___ Phone ___

Notes ___

Reception Estimate Worksheet

	Estimate No. 1		Estimate No. 2		Estimate No. 3	
	Name _____		Name _____		Name _____	
	Phone _____		Phone _____		Phone _____	
	Description	**Cost**	**Description**	**Cost**	**Description**	**Cost**
Site Rental						
Food						
Beverages						
Wedding Cake						
Entertainment						
Equipment: Rental Chairs, Tables, etc.						
Services: Waiters, Waitresses, Bartenders, Parking Valets						
Misc.						
Total						

Reception Site Choice:

Name _____   City _____   Phone _____

Address _____   Person in Charge _____

Notes _____

_____

Planning Checklist

As Soon as Possible
☐ Discuss budget, date and style with fiancé and parents.

☐ Select ceremony and reception sites. Make reservations.

☐ Arrange appointment with officiant.

☐ Start guest list in consultation with fiancé and parents

☐ Choose attendants.

☐ Choose bridal consultant.

☐ Decide on color scheme.

☐ Select wedding attire and accessories.

☐ Experiment with hair style and cut.

☐ Choose mothers' dresses.

☐ Select bridesmaids' gowns.

☐ Select caterer.

☐ Select musicians and/or entertainment. Choose music.

☐ Select photographer and videotape service.

☐ Select florist.

☐ Discuss honeymoon plans. Make reservations.

☐ Order stationery and personalized paper products.

☐ Choose home furnishings.

☐ Enroll at bridal registries.

Three to Four Months Ahead
☐ Complete guest lists.

☐ Begin trousseau shopping. Schedule fittings.

☐ Select wedding ring(s).

☐ Schedule medical appointment for blood tests at least a month in advance of wedding date.

☐ Look for residence.

Six to Eight Weeks Ahead
☐ Select bakery. Order cake.

☐ Order accessories such as ring pillow, guest book, cake knife, garter, candles and decorations.

☐ Arrange for rental equipment.

☐ Address and mail invitations.

☐ Make rehearsal party reservations.

☐ Select gifts for attendants and each other.

☐ Purchase luggage.

☐ Select formalwear for groom's party.

☐ Begin thank-you notes.

☐ Schedule appointment for formal portrait.

One Month Ahead
☐ Apply for marriage license.

☐ Plan bachelor and bachelorette's parties.

☐ Schedule hair and manicure appointments for wedding.

☐ Arrange bridal party transportation.

☐ Arrange valet parking service.

Setting Your Style

Planning Checklist

CONTINUED

☐ Send wedding announcement and glossy photo to newspapers.

☐ Schedule final fittings.

☐ Arrange seating for reception.

☐ Order flowers.

Two Weeks Ahead

☐ Ask mother to confirm reception guest list.

☐ Inform caterer of number.

☐ Check trousseau for last minute needs.

☐ Check bridal attire for fit, comfort and repairs.

One Week Ahead

☐ Confirm details with florist, photographer, musicians, entertainers, caterer, baker, and others.

☐ Confirm rehearsal plans with attendants.

☐ Set aside wedding attire including under-garments, cosmetics, safety pins, needle and thread, tissues, etc.

☐ Prepare for receiving line. Cross check less familiar names with mother.

☐ Check bridal party attire for proper fit.

☐ Address announcements to be mailed wedding day.

☐ Begin packing for honeymoon.

☐ Treat yourself to facial, massage and pedicure. Rest when possible.

Sunday	Monday	Tuesday	Wednesday	Thursday	Friday	Saturday

Notes:

_____

_____

_____

_____

Planning Calendar

Sunday	Monday	Tuesday	Wednesday	Thursday	Friday	Saturday

Notes: _____

_____

_____

_____

Planning Calendar

Sunday	Monday	Tuesday	Wednesday	Thursday	Friday	Saturday

Notes: _____

_____

_____

_____

Planning Calendar

Sunday	Monday	Tuesday	Wednesday	Thursday	Friday	Saturday

Notes: _____

_____

_____

_____

Planning Calendar

Sunday	Monday	Tuesday	Wednesday	Thursday	Friday	Saturday

Notes:

Planning Calendar

Sunday	Monday	Tuesday	Wednesday	Thursday	Friday	Saturday

Notes:

_____

_____

_____

_____

Planning Calendar

Sunday	Monday	Tuesday	Wednesday	Thursday	Friday	Saturday

Notes:

42

Your Bridal Party

Your Bridal Party

Your Bridal Party

Y ou've set the date and the budget and chosen the style. Now you and he should think about how many attendants you want and who they'll be.

Don't go overboard and ask all your friends. Be selective. Too often, brides-to-be give in to feelings of obligation and end up with some attendants who don't "fit." Choose close friends and family members who are special to you.

Choosing Attendants

Bride's Party

Customarily, 12 bridesmaids are the limit but you can have any number, even or uneven. In the latter case, pair off some in the processional and have the rest walk single file. When bridesmaids outnumber ushers in the recessional, the extras can pair up or walk singly.

Your maid and/or matron of honor is usually the one you feel closest to — your sister perhaps, or close friend. Brides generally choose good friends and close family members, a cousin, for instance, for bridesmaids. Pregnancy is no barrier these days. Just choose a bridesmaid gown that's flattering to her. It's a nice gesture to ask your groom's sister to symbolize the joining of your families.

Younger sisters or cousins, between 10 and 16 years old, can be junior bridesmaids with responsibilities similar to the others.

Groom's Party

The best man traditionally is the groom's brother or closest friend. But he may decide to ask his father, grandfather, uncle, or son if he's been married before. Ushers, similarly, are close friends and relatives. Again, it's gracious to ask a man from your family to join the men's group. Choose the number you want using one usher to 50 guests as a guide only. They can be paired or walk singly during the processional.

Host's Aide

Where bridal consultants might be thought of as stage managers, it's always wise to have house managers to see that the "audience" is attended to. Have one or two relatives or close friends greet guests and entertain them while you're busy, show them where to put their coats, and see that they sign the guest book. Ask them to help in the kitchen, serve the food, or clean up afterwards. Recognize this effort with a note and a little gift.

Child Attendants

Young children, between the ages of four and eight, usually serve as flower girl or boy, ring-bearer, trainbearer, or page. They undeniably add charm to a ceremony although they may require special attention to help overcome nervousness and insure good behavior. Sometimes it's surprising how formal clothes change little devils into perfect angels.

Let them skip the rehearsal dinner for a good night's sleep. And have their parents at the wedding to reassure them. Young attendants sit with their parents at the reception or at a special children's table with an adult close by.

You'll find easy-to-use worksheets on the following pages to list your attendants.

Bride's Attendants List

Maid of Honor

Address

City   Phone

Duties

Matron of Honor

Address

City   Phone

Duties

Bridesmaid

Address

City   Phone

Duties

Bridesmaid

Address

City   Phone

Duties

Bridesmaid

Address

City   Phone

Duties

Bridesmaid

Address

City   Phone

Duties

Bridesmaid

Address

City   Phone

Duties

Bridesmaid

Address

City   Phone

Duties

Bride's Attendants List

Junior Bridesmaid _____

Address _____

City _____ Phone _____

Duties _____

Junior Bridesmaid _____

Address _____

City _____ Phone _____

Duties _____

Flower Girl _____

Address _____

City _____ Phone _____

Duties _____

Flower Girl _____

Address _____

City _____ Phone _____

Duties _____

Aide _____

Address _____

City _____ Phone _____

Duties _____
_____
_____

Aide _____

Address _____

City _____ Phone _____

Duties _____
_____
_____
_____
_____
_____

Notes _____

Groom's Attendants List

Best Man _____   City _____ Phone _____

Address _____   Duties _____

Usher _____   Usher _____

Address _____   Address _____

City _____ Phone _____   City _____ Phone _____

Duties _____   Duties _____

Usher _____   Usher _____

Address _____   Address _____

City _____ Phone _____   City _____ Phone _____

Duties _____   Duties _____

Usher _____   Usher _____

Address _____   Address _____

City _____ Phone _____   City _____ Phone _____

Duties _____   Duties _____

Ringbearer _____   Trainbearer or Page _____

Address _____   Address _____

City _____ Phone _____   City _____ Phone _____

Duties _____   Duties _____

Your Bridal Party

Who Does What

Don't let the numerous details of your wedding overwhelm you. Planning well in advance if possible is the key. Always keep in mind that your wedding day should be fun for you, too. Turn to a bridal consultant for help. And delegate, delegate. You don't have to make every decision. Let members of the bridal party make less important ones. But, never forget you're the conductor of your wedding symphony.

In the past, everyone had a well-defined area of responsibility. Now with modern mobility, career obligations and scattered families, you and your fiancé, along with parents, have to decide what's best for you. Start with the traditional ways and reshape them to your own style.

Groom

He chooses his own attendants, of course, and selects their gifts; keeps his family updated on all developments; buys the engagement and wedding rings; and arranges the honeymoon. Some brides like to be surprised, many more prefer a say in the decisions. In general, he keeps an eye on his attendants' activities and helps you as much as possible.

Maid/Matron of Honor

She is your right-hand woman, the one you'll turn to for many things: addressing invitations perhaps, recording your gifts, or supervising the bridesmaids' fittings. (If you're having both maid and matron, you'll have double help!) She'll hold your bouquet during the ceremony, act as your official witness and unofficially calm your nerves on many occasions. Usually, the maid of honor takes precedence in the wedding march and is seated in a place of honor at the reception. In the absence of a trainbearer, she'll rearrange your train before the recessional. Ask her to collect your wedding attire after you leave for the honeymoon.

Best Man

He sees that many things run smoothly from the ushers' functions and safe delivery of honeymoon luggage, to offering moral support when the groom sags. Generally, the best man holds the rings, license and travel tickets in safe keeping; pays the officiant's fee; and acts as toastmaster at the bridal table. Suggest that the groom ask him to make honeymoon arrangements and return the groom's formalwear.

Bridesmaids

They certainly add to the pageantry but have few traditional duties. You'll want to include them in all the pre-wedding festivities and call on them for help whenever possible. Have them fill cups with rice, confetti, or rose petals ready to toss for the getaway, or wrap small gifts for the reception guests, like almonds in lace. Bridesmaids help the ushers decorate the getaway car, usually without prompting.

Ushers

They, too, are resources throughout the planning. On the big day, ushers make the first impression on arriving guests so have them well rehearsed. Ushers greet arrivals at the ceremony, ask which family they represent and seat them properly. It adds to the formality of the day when an usher offers his arm to a woman guest. Drop a hint that ushers dance with all the women at a small reception.

Flower Girls

These enchanting tots usually precede the bride and traditionally strew flower petals in her path. But more than one bride has slipped on them, so provide her with paper petals or a basket of fresh flowers instead.

Ringbearer

Usually male, the ringbearer walks in the processional carrying the ring, or a substitute, tied to a ribbon on a satin pillow.

Page or Trainbearer

Like the flower girl and ringbearer, this attendant's major function (except to carry the bridal gown train) is to be adorable.

Your Mother

She'll be your indispensable aide, helping with decisions, advice and shopping whenever she can. Unless she's walking down the aisle with you,

Who Does What

CONTINUED

your mother will be the last person seated before the ceremony and the first to be escorted up the aisle after. As the official host, she'll head the receiving line.

Your Father

Dad escorts you down the aisle to give away his beloved daughter though many brides nowadays prefer to walk alone. Fathers have been heard to complain that they feel left out of wedding preparations. Do you want to make him feel important to you? Ask him to handle the photography arrangements. Or hire the musicians.

Groom's Parents

They will participate according to their proximity, financial involvement and closeness to your family. Suggest your party-givers include them whenever possible. Some groom's parents offer to host the rehearsal party — a welcome respite for you.

Gift Ideas

Bride and Groom's Attendants

☐ Stationery

☐ Appointment book

☐ Gold or silver jewelry/lighter

☐ Silk scarf or tie

☐ Perfume/cologne/toiletries

☐ Jewelry box

☐ Recipe file/hardcover cookbook

☐ Makeup lamp/compact with light

☐ Silk or porcelain flowers in bud vase

☐ Wallet

☐ Money clip/key chain

☐ Tool kit/auto emergency kit

☐ Travel kit

☐ Swiss Army knife

☐ Stadium blanket/thermal picnicware

☐ Coffee mug set

☐ Book

☐ Desk accessories

☐ Pen and pencil set

☐ Gift certificate for restaurant or department store

☐ Comb and brush set

☐ Subscription to magazine

☐ Lamp/decorative accessories

Your Bridal Party

Child Attendants

☐ Games/toys/puzzles

☐ Framed photo of child with newlyweds

☐ Jewelry

☐ Fancy, filled candy jar

☐ Stuffed animal

☐ Gift certificate to favorite store

☐ Circus/concert/or ice show tickets

☐ Record album/cassette

☐ Coin bank

Parents

☐ Thank-you dinner

☐ Theatre or concert tickets

☐ Plant in decorative container

☐ Framed wedding photo

☐ Laminated or framed invitation

☐ Fruit, cheese, or wine basket

☐ Personalized bottle of wine

☐ Calligrapher-written poem or thank-you note

☐ Singing telegram

Gifts for Each Other

☐ Scented massage oil

☐ Surprise candlelight dinner

☐ Tickets to favorite entertainment

☐ Precious metal or stone-set jewelry

☐ Outdoor or at-home clothing

Party Game Prizes

☐ Small potted plant

☐ Decorative candy or nut-filled jar

☐ Crystal or ceramic bud vase

☐ Cologne /toiletries

☐ Book of poems

☐ Cookbook

☐ Notepaper

☐ Miniature picture frame

☐ Gift certificate

☐ Decorative tin box

☐ Record album/cassette

Planning for Out-of-town Guests

When your guests travel to be present because they think your wedding is important, show them how much you appreciate it. Arrange accommodations at a friend's house or a convenient hotel. You're not obliged to pay their expenses but that's up to you. At any rate, ask if group rates are available and whether rooms can be reserved in a block. It's more fun if they're together. Send a map for the ceremony and reception sites along with the formal invitation. And send maps of the city and tourist attractions if their stay will be long enough.

Make a point of entertaining them or ask a friend to host an informal get-together or perhaps a brunch before the wedding. Ask friends to ''adopt a guest'' and see to it they're kept busy and have someone to introduce them around at the reception.

Guest Accommodations List

Name of Hotel/Motel

Address

City   Phone

Rates

Name(s) of Guest(s)

Date Arriving   Date Departing

Reservations Made

Name of Motel/Hotel

Address

City   Phone

Rates

Name(s) of Guest(s)

Date Arriving   Date Departing

Reservations Made

Name of Hotel/Motel

Address

City   Phone

Rates

Name(s) of Guest(s)

Date Arriving   Date Departing

Reservations Made

Name of Motel/Hotel

Address

City   Phone

Rates

Name(s) of Guest(s)

Date Arriving   Date Departing

Reservations Made

Name of Hotel/Motel

Address

City   Phone

Rates

Name(s) of Guest(s)

Date Arriving   Date Departing

Reservations Made

Name of Motel/Hotel

Address

City   Phone

Rates

Name(s) of Guest(s)

Date Arriving   Date Departing

Reservations Made

Questions for the '90s

Questions for the '90s

Divorced Parents

This may be an awkward moment for you and them. The most important guiding principle should be consideration for everybody's feelings. Each situation is unique. How you approach it depends on your relations with parents and stepparents. Discuss your feelings and theirs, remain sensitive and fine tune the arrangements so each one may participate with grace. Remember, the divorce is a reality and the success of your wedding is the goal.

In general, you'll find the right solution by considering your bond with each one and in particular who is sponsoring the wedding. If they're irreconcilably hostile to each other, you'll simply have to separate them. But that's unusual. Most loving parents overcome their personal feelings for the good of their child.

Receptions are less structured so that any arrangement which puts people at ease is acceptable. Guidelines are helpful though for seating at the ceremony.

If they are divorced but not remarried, congenial parents sit together in the left front row at Christian weddings; the reverse at Jewish ceremonies. Otherwise, your mother sits there and your father in the third row on the left.

When each parent has remarried, your mother sits in the customary place with her husband, your father sits with his wife in the third left-hand row.

If you live with your father and stepmother who are sponsoring the wedding, they sit in the front row. Your mother and her husband, honored guests, sit in the third left-hand row.

If your brother or uncle takes the place of your absent father, he sits with your mother. The same would apply to anyone substituting for your mother.

Seat your groom's divorced parents in right-hand rows using the same general guidelines.

Second Marriage

The older we get the more complicated life seems to become and second weddings are no exception. Personal relationships are often more involved — children from the first marriage, friends of the first couple, former in-laws — but with tact and consideration you'll find a way around any problem that rears its ugly head.

This is a general planning guide to follow: second weddings should not appear to compete with, or duplicate, the first. That said, you can be as traditional or innovative as you like. For the most part, when both bride and groom are remarrying, the ceremony is small and informal with the bride and her party dressed in elegant but not "bridal" attire. Though that's not always the case. You may opt for a semi-formal or formal wedding.

But what if one of you is marrying for the first time? And suppose he wants an elaborate, traditional wedding while you think quiet simplicity is the answer? Understanding and compromise is the solution, of course, for wedding questions as well as those throughout married life.

On the other hand, complications are balanced by benefits. Financial decisions will be easier since second wedding expenses are usually paid by the couple themselves.

Religious ceremonies, here again, call for early consultation with the clergymember. Recognize that some are reluctant to marry divorced persons and you may have to inquire around.

Stepchildren

Children, yours and his, raise perhaps the most sensitive questions in a second marriage. Be sure to keep them informed of your plans from the outset. Allow them to make decisions where appropriate and give them honored roles in the day's ceremonies and activities.

This will depend on age and reliability but even the smallest tot can stand with you during the ceremony. Teen-aged or adult children can serve as honor attendants. Younger ones can participate as flower girl, or boy, or as ringbearer. If your ceremony will be small without attendants, or you have more children than available roles, make each one responsible for a task: filling champagne glasses, for example, or checking coats at a simple home celebration.

Ask the child his or her preference. The point is the child should be made to feel like an important member of the new family.

Choosing Your Name

Brides used to take their husbands' name automatically. But, in fact, it has always been custom rather than law in this country (except Hawaii). Now women have a greater sense of their own identity. And, in many cases, they've built a professional reputation before marriage. So you may be faced with a question that never occurred to your mother.

Some questions raised by untraditional married names are easily answered. You retain the same legal rights, for instance, whatever you choose. In fact, you have the legal right to use *any* name as long as you can show it wasn't changed for illegal purposes.

You have the social right too though the questions raised here are apt to be more annoying. Some people are puzzled by anything outside their own experience. Yet it's your decision to make.

Questions for the '90s

Talk it over with your fiancé, make your choice and carry on confidently. But decide in the beginning. It's much easier than changing later on.

Traditional Married Name

The old ways are still the most popular. Centuries of custom aid the bride who takes her husband's family name and the path to follow is well defined. Start by using it socially and professionally. As soon as possible, change significant records and documents. Following is a convenient checklist to help you.

It's important to start or maintain your own credit record. Equal credit laws are on the books but you have to do your part. Most brides have a record already. Remember the student loan you struggled to pay? Or your department store and credit card accounts? If you change them, be sure they stay in *your* name even if it's different. Use Mrs. (or Ms.) *Mary* Doe. A credit record is essential if you want to open your own busine'ss, or co-sign a mortgage loan. Maintain your own bank and charge accounts. Or, if you open joint accounts, insist that creditors keep separate credit files in each name.

Retaining Single Name

In a sense, this is the easiest way — no records need changing. Some brides are keeping their family name because it is distinguished or because they are the last in the line. Don't apologize to people who question you. Be gracious and say you have the right to decide how you shall be called. Some brides split the difference, using their husband's name socially but their birth name professionally.

Many hotels cling to old registration habits, a fact to keep in mind if you decide to keep your present name. In fact, in some states it's still illegal for two adults of different sex to register under dissimilar surnames. Urban hotels are less likely to raise the question than quiet places in the countryside, just the type of place many couples choose for a honeymoon.

To be on the safe side now and whenever you travel together domestically, bring along your marriage certificate. Or, consider the advice of one lawyer who recommends signing the register with your name followed by "and husband" or "and wife." Proof of marriage may also be required overseas if you're touring with passports in different names.

Using Both Names

You can strike a compromise of sorts by retaining your single name and adding your husband's, i.e., Mary Doe Smith. But the most complex name change — and some brides are doing it — is the hyphenated name, Mary Doe-Smith. In fact, some grooms are doing it too, becoming John Doe-Smith, or John Smith-Doe.

Announcing Your Preference

Eventually, people will learn your preference through word of mouth but there are more formal ways. Enclose a card with your wedding invitation, or mail one separately, saying:

Mary Doe and John Smith

wish to announce that both

will be retaining their present names

for all legal and social purposes

after their marriage

May 1, 1982

Or announce it more subtly in an at-home card (see Wedding Invitations). Today business people are apt to assume a bride is retaining her single name. If you're making a change, and want to avoid confusion, send a card to associates saying:

Ms. Mary Doe

announces she has adopted the surname of

Smith

Choosing Your Name

CONTINUED

Your wedding announcement in newspapers is another means of reporting name preference.

Checklist for Name Changes

Some agencies, Social Security for one, require your marriage license (or a copy) along with notification. Check by phone before writing:

☐ Driver's license

☐ Car registration

☐ Social Security

☐ Voter's registration

☐ Passport

☐ Bank accounts

☐ Credit cards

☐ Insurance policies

☐ School and/or employer's records

☐ Post office

☐ Employment records

☐ Pension plans

☐ Stocks

☐ Bonds

☐ Property titles

☐ Leases

☐ Wills

☐ Beneficiaries

(**Resource:** Center for a Women's Own Name, 261 Kimberly, Barrington, IL 60010; Lucy Stone's, San Francisco, CA.)

The Older Bride

You've asked yourself this question and decided the answer is no. Here you are, a successful career woman, approaching 50 and in love with a wonderful man. Does your wedding have to be different?

The older bride is claiming as her own most of the time-honored wedding traditions. Although you may decide to forgo some of the less dignified social practices, your gown can be as elaborate or simple as you choose. Long white dresses are popular, worn with a simple veil and headpiece or a flattering hat. Have attendants dress in elegant clothes and ask a close friend to escort you down the aisle.

Your wedding is as special as any other. Plan it in your own style. Since you and he have been on your own for many years, you'll probably be paying your own wedding expenses and won't have any obligation to consult with and reach compromises with others.

Reaffirming Vows

Marry in haste, repent in leisure, they used to say. Now, if you marry in haste and later regret that you missed all the ceremony and celebration, just retrace your steps and start over again.

Renew your vows, or have a special blessing, in an elaborate church setting with all the bridal trimmings and have a big bash afterwards. Formalities, such as printed invitations, would be in order when the second service follows close upon the first. However, after a few months have passed these conventions are not used.

Most people feel a gift is not necessary under the circumstances but, if you receive one, the same courteous note is expected.

The custom of reaffirming vows many years after the wedding is gaining in popularity too. Often, the occasion is a special anniversary, the silver or the golden perhaps. The couple's children (and sometimes grandchildren) take part in the ceremony along with other family members and friends. The original vows are repeated or something special is written for the ceremony which is held in a religious setting or in the family home. A gala party often follows.

Your Place, My Place, or Ours

When, after years of making their own decisions, two independent people pledge to share life together, it takes more than love to make a successful merger. Among other things, it takes tolerance, negotiation and mutual respect.

Every marriage begins with a power struggle of some kind. It may be over conflicting claims to the left side of the bed. Or it may be dead serious: for example, which home is closed down.

The ideal solution is to find a happy compromise for each dispute. Sounds simple, doesn't it? But it isn't simple because the struggle is really about control — control over one's identity. If satisfactory answers aren't found, sometimes the only solution is divorce.

A test of marital compatibility begins when you try merging two households. Few of us are able, or even desire, to start from scratch with everything new. We become attached to things. Still, it would be best to move the old things into a brand-new home. This avoids conflicts over issues of territoriality. On top of that, a new home is not haunted by memories of a former spouse or lover.

But, while this may be preferable, financial considerations often scotch the idea. You may have no choice but for one of you to move into the other's one-bedroom apartment. Now your skills at compromise will be tested to the limit. Forced to retrench in order to share a closet, you'll find every last blouse you own is indispensable.

Take comfort. There's nothing like a crisis to impose order. Space can be expanded by using it more efficiently. Before you merge wardrobes and coffee mugs, look around in closet shops for space-saving devices; call in a carpenter to build shelves; browse through magazines for the latest ideas for using every inch to its maximum effectiveness.

Next, deal with the furniture decisions. Each of you draw up an inventory, listing every piece in a yes, no, or maybe column. As the no column grows, you'll have a clear picture of the disposable items. Compare lists and make compromises one by one until only controversial items are left. You might as well toss coins for these.

Children, especially children of divorce, are an important factor in housing decisions. They need reassurance. It may prove wiser for the health of your marriage to live in the same home the children are familiar with, in spite of its drawbacks, at least until they feel more secure.

Pre-Nuptial Agreements

Today many couples are choosing to sign agreements before they are married. These outline what each individually owned before the wedding, and specify arrangements in the unfortunate event of a dissolution of the marriage.

This can be a very touchy and personal matter which should be discussed and agreed upon months before the ceremony. You may want to have an attorney draw up an agreement. If it appears to be a simple agreement, do it yourselves. Be sure to have it witnessed or notarized. This is an optional agreement and depends on the individual needs and desires of every couple.

How to Handle the Extras

Storage

Some surplus items are not disposable and should be stored for the time being.

Before you accept anyone's kind offer of free attic space, check for signs of dampness and cramped spaces through which large pieces won't pass. Even where no dampness is suspected, books, mattresses and wooden furniture should be well-wrapped in plastic to avoid mold or mildew. Buy a desiccant (moisture-absorber) in a hardware store to place in boxes and drawers. Build a wooden platform, if necessary, to prevent any item touching a basement floor.

Some large cities have places that rent individual, concrete, self-storage units. These garage-like structures have sprinklers and are accessible to the renter only. You must do your own packing and hauling. However, this is a relatively inexpensive way to buy storage space. Many are well-lighted and fenced with closed-circuit TV security systems and sometimes, guard dogs.

At a greater cost, storage and moving companies will relieve you of all the work. They'll pack everything expertly in your home and move it to their warehouse. The cost for these services is high; the monthly storage charge considerably less. Any reputable company will give you an estimate of the cost which is figured on the higher charge of either cubic footage or weight.

Auctions

Auction sales offer several possibilities depending on the type of item you're selling. A licensed auctioneer will evaluate what you have and hold a sale in the home if the profit potential is attractive enough. The owner gets a percentage of total sales. Be sure to ask who has the responsibility for advertising the auction.

Prestigious houses like Sotheby-Parke Bernet take valuable articles on consignment to be put up for sale according to the schedule they set. They won't consider selling the contents of a home unless its a well-known showplace.

Other less-exclusive auction houses will sell an entire household by the lot or by the item.

Charitable Contributions

The Internal Revenue Service allows deductions for donations to recognized charities. Check first with them for the organization's tax status. If it is approved, ask for an evaluation of your donations and a receipt for the total value. You must itemize deductions on your tax return to take advantage of this.

Yard, Garage and Tag Sales

Check first to find out whether a license is required. Spread the word by placing posters on telephone poles at major intersections in the area, in the lobby or laundry room of your apartment house and in the local newspaper. Publications often accept such ads at no cost to you. If you have too few items, talk with neighbors about joining forces.

Neither Borrower Nor Lender Be

Shakespeare was right. Too often, the things we lend our friends or relatives become their permanent possessions. If the article has sentimental value to you or you have plans to use it in the future, pay for the cost of storage rather than lend it. Otherwise, give it away to a friend or a deserving community service agency, a youth club perhaps or a senior citizen center.

Your Wedding Stationery

*I*nvitations set the tone of your wedding. They tell guests in advance what style you've chosen for the celebration. Select them, and all your wedding stationery, with care so they reflect the importance you place on the day.

Contemporary brides are so strongly influenced by tradition, it's not surprising to find that many tread the tried and true path. Customary formal invitation styles are still widely used. The difference now is that innovative modes are in too. Be a nonconformist — have yours written by a calligrapher, or custom designed.

A handwritten note on personalized stationery may strike just the right note for a small informal wedding. More often, brides use the printed invitations found at stationers, printers and department stores. Prices vary — comparison shop.

Addressing

*A*ddresses should always be hand written, using black ink, in a neat, legible script. You might recruit a friend with superior penmanship, or use a calligrapher. The outside envelope is for the names and address, of principal family members. On the inside envelope, repeat those names and add underneath the first names of minor children. No address is needed. Send separate invitations to guests over 16, addressed to Ms., Miss, Misses, Mr. or Messrs. Call the post office for zip codes or stop by to use their directory.

Formal titles, such as Doctor, Captain and The Reverend, are written out, although the usual Ms., Mr. and Mrs. are abbreviated.

Many married women nowadays prefer being addressed by their professional names and titles. In this case, send one invitation with her full name written above his. Unrelated roommates receive separate invitations as do the dates of single friends (ask your friend for the address).

Wedding Guest List

Name	Address	City	State	Telephone	No. Invited
1					
2					
3					
4					
5					
6					
7					
8					
9					
10					
11					
12					
13					
14					
15					
16					
17					
18					
19					
20					
21					
22					
23					
24					
25					
26					

Wedding Guest List

Name	Address	City	State	Telephone	No. Invited
27					
28					
29					
30					
31					
32					
33					
34					
35					
36					
37					
38					
39					
40					
41					
42					
43					
44					
45					
46					
47					
48					
49					
50					
51					
52					

Wedding Guest List

Name	Address	City	State	Telephone	No. Invited
53					
54					
55					
56					
57					
58					
59					
60					
61					
62					
63					
64					
65					
66					
67					
68					
69					
70					
71					
72					
73					
74					
75					
76					
77					
78					

Wedding Guest List

Name	Address	City	State	Telephone	No. Invited
79					
80					
81					
82					
83					
84					
85					
86					
87					
88					
89					
90					
91					
92					
93					
94					
95					
96					
97					
98					
99					
100					
101					
102					
103					
104					

Wedding Guest List

Name	Address	City	State	Telephone	No. Invited
105					
106					
107					
108					
109					
110					
111					
112					
113					
114					
115					
116					
117					
118					
119					
120					
121					
122					
123					
124					
125					
126					
127					
128					
129					
130					

Your Wedding Stationery

Invitations

Traditional Wording

Mr. and Mrs. Alexander Cole
request the honour of your presence
at the marriage of their daughter
Ms. Rachel Cole
to
Mr. Mark Jackson
Sunday, the sixth of June
Nineteen hundred and eighty-two
at three o'clock
All Saints Church
Los Angeles, California

RSVP by the twenty-second of May
Nineteen hundred and eighty-two

Groom's Parents

Mr. and Mrs. Jason Jackson
request the honour of your presence
at the marriage of
Rachel Cole
to their son
Mark Jackson

Invitations

Bride and Groom's Parents

Mr. and Mrs. Alexander Cole
and
Mr. and Mrs. Jason Jackson
request the honour of your presence
at the marriage of their children
Rachel Cole
to
Mark Jackson

Divorced Parents (depending on who hosts)

Mr. and Mrs. Alexander Cole
or
Mr. Alexander Cole
or
Mrs. Smith Cole
or (if parents have remarried)
Mr. and Mrs. Alexander Cole
and
Mr. and Mrs. Charles Miller

Bride and Groom

The honour of your presence
is requested at the marriage of
Rachel Cole
to
Mark Jackson

Invitations

CONTINUED

Contemporary Wording

Mr. and Mrs. Alexander Cole
would like you to
join with their daughter
Rachel
and
Mark Jackson
in their celebration of love

—
or
—

Rachel Cole
and
Mark Jackson
invite you to share the joy
of the beginning of their new life together
when on Sunday, the sixth of June
at three o'clock
they exchange marriage vows

—
or
—

Please join our family
on the joyous occasion
when our daughter, Rachel
will be married to Mark Jackson
on Sunday, the sixth of June
at three o'clock
All Saints Church
Los Angeles, California
Your presence in the celebration of love
will be of special importance to all of us
Mary and Alexander Cole

Reception Cards

When all guests are invited to the ceremony and reception, one invitation will serve the purpose by adding:

Reception immediately following
Beachview Hotel
13933 Pacific Coast Highway
Marina del Rey

For a select number of reception guests, enclose a separate card. This is usually about half the size and identical in typeface, paper and printing style. Enclose a map for less well-known locations. The card should read:

Reception
immediately following the ceremony
Beachview Hotel
13933 Pacific Coast Highway
Marina del Rey

—
or
—

Breakfast celebration
to follow ceremony
Beachview Hotel
13933 Pacific Coast Highway
Marina del Rey

Your Wedding Stationery

Response Cards

A response card enclosed with the invitation is not necessary. But it's a nice touch and a good way to keep track. Don't assume a guest is not coming if you don't hear. Have someone call to verify, preferably the host.

Within the Ribbons / Reserved Section Cards

*O*ften a section is set apart, at large weddings, for close friends and relatives. Then a card should be enclosed, handwritten or printed, saying: "Bride's (or Groom's) Section," or "Within the Ribbons," or enclose a pew card with the number.

Announcements

*S*end announcements to people who live too far away, to those you're unable to include in a small wedding, when you feel an invitation would imply an obligation to send a gift, or after an elopement. Consult your stationer for advice on the wording.

At Home Cards

*T*hese cards are often enclosed with an announcement. Today it's a good way to tell people when you're keeping your maiden or professional name. It could read:

Mr. and Mrs. Mark Jackson
or
Mr. Mark Jackson
and
Ms. Rachel Cole
after the ninth of September
1586 North Main Street
Glendale, Califonia 90678

Thank-you Notes

*G*enerally, thank-you notes are written on small folded cards which have your married name or initials printed on the front and blank message space inside. It's better for you, and certainly more courteous, to send one as soon as the gift arrives. Tell the sender you're looking forward to seeing him or her at the wedding. Some gifts will arrive, no doubt, when you're in the middle of the last minute rush, or off on your honeymoon. A nice touch is to have your mother send printed cards (found at any department store or stationer) saying:

Rachel and Mark sincerely appreciate
your beautiful gift and will take pleasure
in sending you a personal note
sometime soon.

Be sure to mention the gift and why you feel it's special. If it's a thingamabob you can't identify, just try your best to describe it. Don't mention the amount of any money gift — say how you plan to use it.

Sign your maiden name before the wedding, your married name after. Most important, send all your thank-you notes within two months after the wedding. Your friends took the time to select beautiful gifts for you, let them know how much you appreciate them.

Guest Data File

O f course, the fancier your wedding, the more paper work is involved. *Bride Guide* worksheets solve this problem by breaking down the details into workable units. But, in addition, you might find it helpful, especially for a very large wedding, to keep a card file of information about each guest. Pick up 3x5 index cards while you're at the stationer and use the sample below to help you design your own system.

☐ **Bride's Guest**

☐ **Groom's Guest**

☐ Announcement

Invitations   ☐ Ceremony   ☐ Reception   RSVP ☐ Yes ☐ No

Guest's Name _____

Address _____

City _____ State _____ Zip _____

Telephone Number _____

Shower Gift _____

Shower Gift _____

Wedding Gift _____

Check When Thank–You Card Has Been Sent: ☐ Shower 1   ☐ Shower 2   ☐ Wedding

Invitation Keepsakes

H ere are some decorative ideas for preserving your wedding invitation after your ceremony:

• Your invitation can be mounted and framed with a few flowers from your wedding bouquet.

• The wording of your invitation can be embroidered or painted on a lace and satin pillow.

• You can have the wording of your invitation engraved on the lid of a crystal or silver box filled with candy or potpourri.

• You can have the wording of your invitation handpainted or silk screened on a porcelain plate along with your wedding picture.

Bridal Gift Registries

Bridal Gift Registries

Wedding Gifts

How to Use Gift Registries

*I*t just doesn't make sense to keep your fingers crossed and hope your gifts will be what you want. The costs of starting a home are too high. Most stores have a bridal registry and many have wedding consultants as well. Using them assures you two that gifts will be what you want. And they make choices so much easier for the givers. No wild guesses for them and less chance of duplication for you. You're really doing everyone a favor.

It does take organization to use them effectively. But then, as we keep emphasizing, doing it well means planning it well. Start by window shopping together and narrow down your choices. Register your final choices, tell your mother and friends, and the word will get around in no time. In fact, it's common now for shower hosts to add a note to invitations, i.e., ''Gloria is registered at...''

Select one registry — perhaps the simplest way for you — or use several: a linen specialty shop, or a favorite gift store for accessories, above all, department stores where you can list a wide selection of choices and prices. As your gifts arrive, update overlapping registers. Some stores have special phones for this.

Ask the registry consultant for guidance. She'll know all about the store's services and will be an encyclopedia of consumer information. Many consultants keep their bridal customers informed of special sales, fashion shows, decorating seminars, cooking classes, and the like.

Major department stores circulate your register to all their branches, local and national. Also, consider registering with local stores back home to make it easier for those folks still there. These services are free — it makes good sense to use them generously.

Don't be shy about registering some expensive things. Some friends may decide to pool their resources for one big gift. And don't overlook workaday items like kitchen utensils for shower gifts. What counts is a good balance of many choices.

The gift registry's usefulness doesn't stop after the wedding. It may continue to help with holiday gifts for several years. You furnish a home over a period of time, after all. Ask your consultant. Many maintain files for up to five years.

We've included worksheets to help you keep track.

Returning and Exchanging Gifts

*Y*ou've made your choices carefully and registered them in several places, but still you receive duplications or hopelessly inappropriate gifts. Should you rush to tell the giver? Not at all. Send a nice thank-you note and quietly return it for another choice. It's best to wait till the celebrations are over. Then you'll have an overall picture of what you've received and where you need to fill in. Keeping all the tags and inserts will help.

When something arrives damaged, notify the store as soon as possible and ask them *not* to contact the sender. Unless it's insured. In that case, you'll want to tell your friend who can collect the insurance and replace the damaged article.

Some people prefer to know you're exchanging a gift since their first concern is pleasing you. But everyone has an Aunt Susie or Uncle Tom who insists you need Victorian frippery when your taste runs to high tech simplicity. Use common sense and tact. If you're sure feelings will be hurt, keep the white elephant in a closet to be brought out and displayed for each visit. It's a small price to pay for keeping a loved one happy.

Displaying Gifts

Many people feel this practice is outmoded and ostentatious. The trend is away from materialistic values. Our friends often come from different economic levels or age groups; displaying expensive gifts may overshadow modest ones when, in each case, they were given in the same loving spirit.

Gifts of Cash and Other Ideas

Wedding gifts of cash, unless there is an ethnic tradition for it, make some people uncomfortable. The purpose for a gift should be to help the new couple with what they need most. If cash is your first priority, for a down payment on a car, or to help you through the last year of medical school, don't hesitate to let people know.

One altruistic, imaginative bride and groom, well established in their careers, requested that donations be sent in their names to organizations dedicated to improving the environment.

Another couple added the statement "No gifts, please" to the bottom of their invitation. They felt gifts would be inappropriate in their situation; their friends knew just what to do — or not to do.

Here are some unusual gifts for you to think about:

- An electric or hand-powered ice cream maker.
- A hammock woven in a remote South American Indian village — or the sturdy camping variety.
- Reference books: dictionary, thesaurus or atlas.
- Any beautiful, hardcover, quality book.
- An enormous, or rare, house plant.
- Adult games made of luxurious leather or ivory.
- An exotic bird in its own cage.
- A wine rack filled with favored varieties.
- Garden or hand tools of superior quality.

- A pair of bicycles, sleeping bags, or a toboggan.
- Educational gifts: double tuition for a college course or foreign language class.
- An antique rocking chair, weathervane or clock.
- A contemporary work of art.
- A handmade weaving or wall hanging by a favorite artist.
- An exercycle.
- Stocks, bonds, or mutual fund shares.

Anniversary Gift Chart

	Traditional	Modern
1st	paper	clocks
2nd	cotton	china
3rd	leather	crystal and glass
4th	linen	electric appliance
5th	wood	silverware
6th	iron	wood
7th	wool	desk set
8th	bronze	linens and lace
9th	pottery	leather
10th	tin, aluminum	diamond jewelry
11th	steel	fashion jewelry, accessories
12th	silk	pearl or colored gem
13th	lace	textile and fur
14th	ivory	gold jewelry
15th	crystal	watches
16th	—	sterling or plate, silver hollowware
17th	—	furniture
18th	—	porcelain
19th	—	bronze
20th	china	platinum
25th	silver	sterling silver jubilee
30th	pearl	diamond
35th	coral, jade	jade
40th	ruby	ruby
45th	sapphire	sapphire
50th	gold	golden jubilee
55th	emerald	emerald
60th	diamond	diamond

Gift Registry Worksheet

Formal Dinnerware

_____ _____

_____ _____

_____ _____

_____ _____

_____ _____

_____ _____

Formal Dinnerware

_____ _____

_____ _____

_____ _____

_____ _____

_____ _____

_____ _____

Informal Dinnerware

_____ _____

_____ _____

_____ _____

_____ _____

_____ _____

_____ _____

Informal Dinnerware

_____ _____

_____ _____

_____ _____

_____ _____

_____ _____

_____ _____

Sterling Flatware

_____ _____

_____ _____

_____ _____

_____ _____

_____ _____

_____ _____

Sterling Flatware

_____ _____

_____ _____

_____ _____

_____ _____

_____ _____

_____ _____

Stores Registered at: **Phone**

_____ _____

_____ _____

Stores Registered at: **Phone**

_____ _____

_____ _____

Stainless Flatware

_____   _____
_____   _____
_____   _____
_____   _____
_____   _____
_____   _____

Crystal

_____   _____
_____   _____
_____   _____
_____   _____
_____   _____
_____   _____

Casual Glassware

_____   _____
_____   _____
_____   _____
_____   _____
_____   _____
_____   _____

Stores Registered at: **Phone**

_____   _____
_____   _____

Stainless Flatware

_____   _____
_____   _____
_____   _____
_____   _____
_____   _____
_____   _____

Crystal

_____   _____
_____   _____
_____   _____
_____   _____
_____   _____
_____   _____

Casual Glassware

_____   _____
_____   _____
_____   _____
_____   _____
_____   _____
_____   _____

Stores Registered at: **Phone**

_____   _____
_____   _____

Gift Registry Worksheet

Kitchen Accessories

_____ _____
_____ _____
_____ _____
_____ _____
_____ _____
_____ _____

Housewares

_____ _____
_____ _____
_____ _____
_____ _____
_____ _____
_____ _____

Bathroom Accessories

_____ _____
_____ _____
_____ _____
_____ _____
_____ _____
_____ _____

Bedroom Accessories

_____ _____
_____ _____
_____ _____
_____ _____
_____ _____
_____ _____

Extra Comforts

_____ _____
_____ _____
_____ _____
_____ _____
_____ _____
_____ _____

Home Entertainment:

_____ _____
_____ _____
_____ _____
_____ _____
_____ _____
_____ _____

Bedroom Color(s) _____

Bathroom Color(s) _____

Kitchen Color(s) _____

Other _____

Gift Registry Worksheet

Linens:

Outdoor Accessories:

Electric Appliances:

Sports Equipment:

Luggage:

Misc.

Other

Everyone Loves a Party

Everyone Loves a Party

Everyone Loves a Party

Everything about preparing for a wedding is exciting. The most fun, though, is the round of parties. Nobody needs to justify a party, ever, but wedding parties are usually built around a practical or symbolic theme. Have as many as energy and budget permit. However, two types are standard: bridal showers and "last fling before settling down" parties. We call them the bachelorette party and bachelor party. They're also known as the bride's party and groom's party.

Bridal Showers

Tradition decrees that only friends, never family, give showers. Well, like so many rules these days, that no longer holds. Our contacts are so much broader these days than our grandmother's were, that often several different people plan a series of showers. If you catch wind of it, try suggesting that each shower have a different guest list: for example, one for business friends, another for old school pals and a third for relatives. Even so, your attendants and close relatives may receive several invitations. That can be hard on anyone's pocket-book, especially those who have ceremony expenses too. Let it be known you hope they come to every party but would prefer they bring a gift to only one.

Another trend flying in the face of the traditional all-female party, is the unisex shower, which is really just another Saturday night party — with gifts. Men and women friends present the couple with things they can use together, like games, sports equipment, or a stereo.

But the customary shower is for women only. Although the groom usually shows up at the end of the party. This type of shower allows you some time to have a little fun with just your close friends and relatives. Theme parties are more popular these days because they are so practical. And shower games really do highlight the program.

When opening your gifts, ask someone to make a list of who gave you what so your thank-you notes will be correct. Tie all the ribbons and bows together, into a bouquet, and save them for a beautiful momento of your shower.

Shower Themes

The theme can be built around anything the newlyweds could use. Gifts are usually less expensive household items, although a group of friends may pitch in for something more costly. There are no rules about the hour or the refreshments; anything from morning coffee to after-dinner dessert is suitable. Hosts often phone invitations or, more commonly, send printed invitations mentioning the theme. Some of the more popular ones are:

Kitchen
Most often-used theme because of the wide variety of inexpensive items a new married couple needs. Ideas range from homely necessities like brooms to linens, cookware, spice racks or a kitchen clock. A food processor, for example, is a good joint gift. Choose your color scheme early and gifts will blend in.

Lingerie/Personal
May include nightgowns and other lingerie or personal items like a makeup mirror, jewelry box or anything you will use for personal grooming — scented bath soap perhaps.

Recreation for Two
Both sexes make up the guest list. Gifts could include computer games, stereo components, recordings or season tickets to the symphony. Outdoor types would love camping equipment, snorkel or scuba equipment, perhaps RV accessories.

Plants
Nothing makes a house feel more like home than greenery. Also, plant accessories such as decorative pottery, plant stands and macrame holders make good gifts.

Bathroom

Monogrammed towels, throw rugs, coordinated tissue box and drinking glass, waste basket and scales are some suggestions for this theme. To repeat, choosing your color scheme early will help.

Bedroom

Aside from the essentials, bedrooms tend to get decorated last. Necessities like sheets, blankets and comforters are appreciated, of course, but so are a clock radio, closet accessories, a door mirror, or a painting.

Shower Games

You Tell Me Quiz

Fill numbered paper cups with soap powder, flour, talcum powder, salt, sugar, baking powder, ground cloves and baking soda. Keep a record of numbers and contents. Blindfold the guests and pass the cups for taste and smell tests. Whoever guesses the most wins.

Scrambled Words

List scrambled words on a large piece of cardboard. Use words associated with weddings, such as marriage (ragimaer), kiss (siks), cake (aeck), garter (rtgare), or the bride and groom's names. Set a time limit and give a prize for the most correct solutions.

The Memory Game

Place small, household items on a tray and cover with a towel. Gather guests in a circle, pass out pencil and paper and uncover the tray. At the end of ten or fifteen seconds, remove the tray and see who can remember the greatest number. Use familiar things: pencil, eraser, nail file, ash tray, matches. Ten or 12 items should be the limit.

Guess Best

Fill a jar with sour balls, beans, chocolate kisses or jelly beans. Have the guests write their guesses of the total number on paper. The closest guess wins.

Pin the Boutonniere

Draw the groom's silhouette on a large piece of cardboard and attach a blowup of his face. Blindfold the guests, turn each around twice, and point towards the picture. See who pins the boutonniere (real or artificial) closest to his lapel.

Bride's Bingo

Purchase this game at a stationery store. It's similar to standard Bingo except that words and phrases are related to weddings. Or have a clever person make the cards and playing pieces.

Bride's Bloopers

While the bride opens her gifts, inconspicuously record all her comments. Read them out loud later on for a good laugh.

Small, inexpensive prizes for the winners add to the fun. Use the handy shower guest lists on the next pages to remember the party details.

Shower I Guest List

Date of Shower _____   **Phone** _____

Time _____   **Location** _____

Hostess(es) _____   **Theme** _____

Name	Address	City	Phone
1			
2			
3			
4			
5			
6			
7			
8			
9			
10			
11			
12			
13			
14			
15			
16			
17			
18			
19			
20			
21			

Shower I Guest List

Name	Address	City	Phone
22			
23			
24			
25			
26			
27			
28			
29			
30			
31			
32			
33			
34			
35			
36			
37			
38			
39			
40			
41			
42			
43			
44			
45			
46			
47			

Shower II Guest List

Date of Shower _____ **Phone** _____

Time _____ **Location** _____

Hostess(es) _____ **Theme** _____

Name	Address	City	Phone
1			
2			
3			
4			
5			
6			
7			
8			
9			
10			
11			
12			
13			
14			
15			
16			
17			
18			
19			
20			
21			

Parties For Attendants

Until now, you and your fiancé have been the stars of the show with your attendants playing secondary roles. Now it's their turn to be honored. In fact, it's a good chance for everyone to relax and let off steam. You've all been rushing around and, historically, all bridal couples admit to last-minute jitters.

Plan these parties a week or two before the wedding. Anyone may host but usually it's the bride and groom. Invite close friends and family, too, if space and finances allow.

This is the one time guests are never expected to bring gifts. But it's a perfect time for the wedding couple to thank their attendants with gifts and review plans for the wedding. Customarily, these gifts are personal articles and attendants who serve the same function, all the ushers, for instance, get the same gifts. Buy different colors or monogram them to make each distinctive. Larger more elaborate weddings may call for more expensive gifts. Never spend so much, however, that you set a standard future couples will have trouble meeting.

A party at home is fine, or at your favorite restaurant, a private club, a local theme park, or any place that's right for a good time. Hot tub parties are popular in Southern California these days. Gone are the days when only bachelor parties tossed convention to the wind. Today, some bridesmaids take the bride to see male exotic dancers.

It's up to you how you want to celebrate your last days as a "single". Some of the old customs seem meaningless today. Many couples, as a matter of fact, are combining two parties in one. It's a good time for attendants to get to know one another and, who knows, it may even be a better party. Some traditions have persisted though. If these sound outdated to you, make up your own.

Bachelorette's Party Tradition

A pink cake is served customarily with a ring or thimble baked into it. The woman who gets the symbol in her piece will be the next bride, so they say.

Bachelor's Party Tradition

The groom signals the end of the party by proposing a champagne toast to his bride. Then the glasses are flung over the shoulder. This assures, we're told, that the glasses will never again be used for a less worthy purpose. The traditional groom's party is held the night before the wedding, almost guaranteeing bleary-eyed males at the ceremony. This custom is phasing out in some places for an evening several days in advance.

Worksheets for the guest lists follow after this suggestion for what may be the most important parties of all.

Parties for Two

With hundreds of details to handle, and your concern for a perfect wedding, the risk is that you and your fiancé may overlook the reason for it all — your commitment to one another.

Take time out of your hectic schedule for romance. Slip off regularly for a cocktail hour together or a barefoot walk along the beach. Rendezvous at an intimate restaurant. Talk about your feelings, your expectations — your joy. Never forget now, or later, that the quality of your time together is the foundation for everything else.

Bachelor Party Guest List

Date _____   Phone _____

Time _____   Location _____

Host _____   _____

Name	Address	Phone
1		
2		
3		
4		
5		
6		
7		
8		
9		
10		
11		
12		
13		
14		
15		
16		
17		
18		
19		
20		
21		

Bachelor Party Guest List

Date _____   **Phone** _____

Time _____   **Location** _____

Host _____   _____

Name	**Address**	**Phone**
1		
2		
3		
4		
5		
6		
7		
8		
9		
10		
11		
12		
13		
14		
15		
16		
17		
18		
19		
20		
21		

Finishing Touches

Ceremony Rehearsal

Scheduling the rehearsal and party the night before the wedding may not be wise. Parties are for relaxation and uninhibited fun. No one counts the toasts, spirits are high and the morning after blahs could be the price you pay. Instead, check with your bridal party members and schedule the runthrough two or three days in advance. Any missing member can be filled in later.

Ask everyone to be prompt and wear casual but appropriate clothing. It's a good idea for you to wear your wedding shoes during the rehearsal to break them in.

Your officiant will help you run through the paces and practice the responses. Don't hesitate to ask questions. When everyone knows exactly what to expect, the ceremony will run smoothly. Be sure the officiant knows correct name pronunciations. Are you wearing a long train? Then walk down the aisle on your father's right or he'll have to step over it to reach the right hand pew. Practice makes perfect so rehearse several times if necessary.

Very young attendants should practice, too. People differ on the best way to handle this. Some say children are more self-confident when they're well-rehearsed; others say once over lightly is enough, repetition will overemphasize their role. You know best how your little friends will react. If you sense that a small tot will fidget once the processional is ended, have him or her join parents until the recessional begins.

Ask your ushers to arrive early and keep the ceremonial wheels turning. Guests should be seated as they arrive to avoid a backup at the door. Discuss seating arrangements — will all the bride's family be on the left, the groom's on the right, or will guests be evenly distributed? Have a list, for the head usher, of guests who'll sit in special sections. And decide if guests will leave at will or follow ushers' directions. Finally, assign certain ushers to arrange the ribbons, unroll the white aisle carpet, collect prayer books after the ceremony and direct guests to the reception.

Rehearsal Party

Anyone may host a rehearsal party although the groom's parents often do. Is the party giver talking about an elaborate formal dinner while you're looking forward to shedding your shoes and relaxing with a sandwich and beer? Talk it over, it's one of the easier questions to answer.

The guest list should include parents and all adult members of the bridal party with their spouses or dates. Ask your child attendants' parents too. Then it's up to you if other friends, grandparents, cousins and others should be invited to join the fun. Even-handedness is what counts here. Don't ask all your cousins, for instance, and none of his. Some brides invite the clergymember and soloist. They are, after all, wedding VIPs. Out-of-town guests, who've missed other festivities, would love to be included.

Give your guest list to the host and suggest that a phone call or casual note would be a perfectly proper invitation. If the hosts live out of town, the groom's parents in particular, let them know you stand ready to help with suggestions for places and services.

The rehearsal party, often the last scheduled gathering before the actual ceremony, is a good time to double check transportation arrangements and receiving line positions.

At the end of this section, are worksheets for recording rehearsal party details and estimates.

Ceremony Seating Plans

Most Christian churches and the Reformed Jewish temples seat the bride's immediate family in the front left hand row, while the front right hand row is reserved for the groom's. The seating is reversed in Conservative and Orthodox Jewish congregations. Customarily, family friends and relatives follow this division. Although, as we've said, you may prefer to balance the appearance.

Instruct your organist to play soft music while the guests are being seated.

Everyone knows the signal that the drama is about to begin. The groom's mother enters, escorted by the best man or one of the ushers, followed by his father. Your mother is the last to be seated in the traditional Christian order. In Jewish ceremonies, both parents customarily escort the bride and groom. A musical fanfare announces that the stately processional is at hand.

Processional Order

According to some traditions, the clergy-member precedes the groom and best man down the aisle. Most Christian churches have them wait at the altar. The procession-al is then led by ushers, in order of height, walking singly or in pairs, and the bridesmaids in a similar arrangement. Customary spacing is six to ten feet apart. Maid and/or matron of honor follow, next the ringbearer, the flower girl, and then all eyes are on you, the center of attention.

Recessional Order

You and your groom lead the joyous reces-sional arm in arm. The bridal party leaves according to religious custom, or in the order you've chosen. Ushers then remove ribbons from reserved sections, escort honored guests up the aisle and indicate whether the others should exit row by row or casually.

Marriage License

One of the constitutional rights that states guard jealously is the responsibility for laws governing legal marriage. There is some agreement among them — they all require licenses, for example. Beyond that, there is much variation from state to state.

In general, marriage laws are concerned with the age of consent, who must give consent for minors to marry, residence and/or citizenship re-quirements, venereal disease control and health protection for subsequent children. There is a waiting period in some states after applying for the license but before it's issued; in some others, after receiving it but before it's valid. In some states, parents' written consent is required for minors to marry, the court must approve in others and both approvals are necessary in a few.

You may know you're over the age of consent but don't count on your word alone. Bring age verification if you think there will be any question. Your birth certificate will do, or baptismal record, naturalization certificate, immigration record, adoption record, or passport. Only certified photo copies are acceptable.

Blood test requirements vary as well. Don't assume that because South Carolina does not re-quire a blood test that North Carolina will have the same law. It doesn't. Where it is required, the test may be just for syphilis, or may include tests for rubella (German measles) and sickle-cell anemia. Blood tests requirements may be waived under certain circumstances.

In states where a residency requirement must be met by one person, the non-resident must satisfy certain laws. You each must apply in person according to some state laws, California for one.

The following chart will help you sort out the laws applying to you. Even with it to refer to, it's a good idea to call or write the county clerk's office to ask for detailed information for your state.

Marriage Information

Source: Compiled by William E. Mariano & Associates,
901 North Broadway, White Plains, N.Y. (as of July 30, 1990)

State*	Minimum Age				Blood test/Physical exam (a)		Wait for license	Wait after license
	With consent		Without consent					
	Men	Women	Men	Women	Required (b)	Other state accepted		
Alabama	14	14	18	18	Yes	Yes	none	none
Alaska	16	16	18	18	Yes	No	3 days	none
Arizona	16	16	18	18	Yes	—	none (d)	none
Arkansas	17	16	18	18	none	—	3 days	none
California	(c)	(c)	18	18	30	Yes	none	none
Colorado	16	16	18	18	Yes	—	none	none
Connecticut	16	16	18	18	35	Yes	4 days	none
Delaware	18	16	18	18	Yes	Yes	none	24 hrs. (h)
District of Columbia	16	16	18	18	30	Yes	3 days	none
Florida	16	16	18	18	60	Yes	3 days	none
Georgia	(c)	(c)	16	16	Yes	Yes	(e)	none
Hawaii	16	16	18	18	Yes	Yes	none	none
Idaho	16	16	18	18	Yes	Yes	(e)	none
Illinois	16	16	18	18	30	Yes	none	1 day
Indiana	17	17	18	18	Yes	No	72 hrs.	none
Iowa	18	18	18	18	Yes	Yes	3 days (d)	none
Kansas	18	18	18	18	Yes	Yes	3 days	none
Kentucky	18	18	18	18	none	—	none	none
Louisiana	18	18	18	18	10	No	none	72 hrs.
Maine	16	16	18	18	none	—	3 days (d)	none
Maryland	16	16	18	18	none	—	48 hrs.	none
Massachusetts	18	18	18	18	33–90	Yes	3 days (d)	none
Michigan	16	16	18	18	30	No	3 days	none
Minnesota	16	16	18	18	none	—	5 days	none
Mississippi	(c)	(c)	17	15	Yes	—	3 days	none
Missouri	15	15	18	18	none	—	3 days	none
Montana	16	16	18	18	6 months	Yes	none	3 days
Nebraska	17	17	17	17	30	Yes	2 days	none
Nevada	16	16	18	18	none	—	none	none
New Hampshire	(c)	(c)	18	18	30	Yes	5 days	none
New Jersey	16	16	18	18	Yes	Yes	72 hrs.	none
New Mexico	16	16	18	18	30	Yes	none	none
New York	16	16	18	18	Yes	No	none	24 hrs. (i)
North Carolina	16	16	18	18	Yes	Yes	(d)	none
North Dakota	16	16	18	18	none	—	none	none
Ohio	18	16	18	18	Yes	Yes	5 days	none
Oklahoma	16	16	18	18	30	No	(e)	none
Oregon	17	17	18	18	none	—	3 days	none
Pennsylvania	16	16	18	18	30	Yes	3 days	none
Rhode Island	18	16	18	18	Yes	No	none	none
South Carolina	16	14	18	18	none	—	24 hrs.	none
South Dakota	16	16	18	18	none	—	none	none
Tennessee	16	16	18	18	Yes	Yes	(e)	none
Texas	14	14	18	18	none	—	none	none
Utah	14	14	18	18	30	Yes	none	none
Vermont	16	16	18	18	30	—	none	3 days
Virginia	16	16	18	18	Yes	Yes (g)	none	none
Washington	17	17	18	18	(f)	—	3 days	none
West Virginia	18	18	18	18	Yes	No	3 days	none
Wisconsin	16	16	18	18	Yes	Yes	5 days	none
Wyoming	16	16	18	18	Yes	Yes	none	none
Puerto Rico	18	16	21	21	Yes	Yes	none	none
Virgin Islands	(c)	(c)	18	18	none	—	8 days	none

*Most states have additional requirements and/or exceptions such as laws for non-residents, and for those under age 21 years and/or the age of consent, laws requiring the filing of notice of intention to marry, and for special situations such as pregnancy, for a minor previously married, and parents of children already born. Individual marriage license clerks may have their own special requirements, especially with respect to proof of age. In addition, marriage laws are constantly changing. Anyone utilizing this chart should consult the local marriage license clerk before making any plans. (a) Different states have different blood test and physical examination requirements. Before trying to use a test or examination from another state, check with the local marriage license clerk. (b) License must be obtained within the number of days indicated after having blood test/physical examination. (c) If younger than age of consent, parties may marry with parental consent and/or judicial approval. (d) Parties must file notice of intention to marry. (e) 3 days if either party is under 18; Georgia, exception if pregnancy or already parents; Oklahoma, 72 hours. (f) Parties must file an affidavit. (g) Must use state form. (h) 24 hours if one or both parties resident of state; 96 hours if both parties are non-residents. (i) Marriage may not be solemnized within 10 days of blood test.

These are examples of traditional religious wedding party formations.

PROCESSIONAL

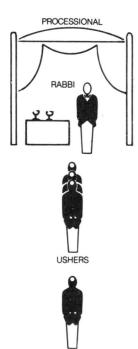

RABBI

USHERS

BEST MAN

GROOM'S FATHER   GROOM'S MOTHER

GROOM

BRIDESMAIDS

MAID OF HONOR

PAGE   FLOWER GIRL

BRIDE'S FATHER

BRIDE

BRIDE'S MOTHER

POSITION AT THE ALTAR

RABBI

BEST MAN   GROOM   BRIDE   MAID OF HONOR

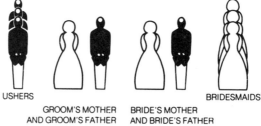

USHERS   GROOM'S MOTHER AND GROOM'S FATHER   BRIDE'S MOTHER AND BRIDE'S FATHER   BRIDESMAIDS

RECESSIONAL

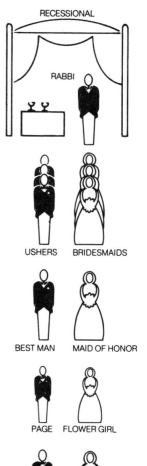

RABBI

USHERS   BRIDESMAIDS

BEST MAN   MAID OF HONOR

PAGE   FLOWER GIRL

GROOM'S FATHER   GROOM'S MOTHER

BRIDE'S FATHER   BRIDE'S MOTHER

GROOM   BRIDE

Christian Ceremony

These are examples of traditional religious wedding party formations.

PROCESSIONAL

OFFICIANT

ALTAR

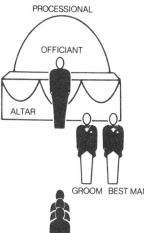

GROOM BEST MAN

USHERS

BRIDESMAIDS

MAID OF HONOR

PAGE RINGBEARER

FLOWER GIRL

FATHER OF BRIDE & BRIDE

POSITION AT THE ALTAR

OFFICIANT

ALTAR

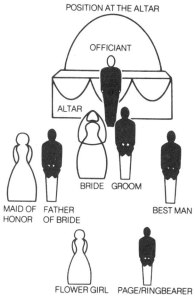

MAID OF   FATHER
HONOR   OF BRIDE   BRIDE   GROOM   BEST MAN

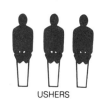

FLOWER GIRL   PAGE/RINGBEARER

BRIDESMAIDS   USHERS

RECESSIONAL

OFFICIANT

ALTAR

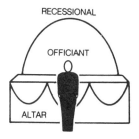

GROOM'S   GROOM'S
MOTHER   FATHER

BRIDE'S   BRIDE'S
MOTHER   FATHER

BRIDESMAIDS   USHERS

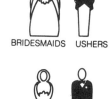

MAID OF HONOR   BEST MAN

FLOWER GIRL   PAGE/RINGBEARER

BRIDE   GROOM

These are examples of traditional religious wedding party formations.

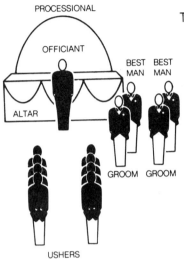

PROCESSIONAL

OFFICIANT

BEST MAN BEST MAN

ALTAR

GROOM GROOM

USHERS

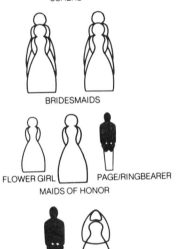

BRIDESMAIDS

FLOWER GIRL PAGE/RINGBEARER

MAIDS OF HONOR

BRIDE'S FATHER ELDER BRIDE

BRIDESMAIDS

FLOWER GIRL PAGE/RING BEARER

MAID OF HONOR

BRIDE'S FATHER YOUNGER BRIDE

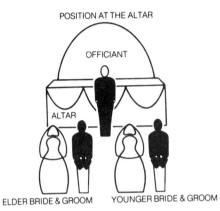

POSITION AT THE ALTAR

OFFICIANT

ALTAR

ELDER BRIDE & GROOM YOUNGER BRIDE & GROOM

MAIDS OF HONOR BEST MEN

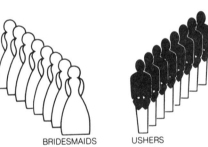

BRIDESMAIDS USHERS

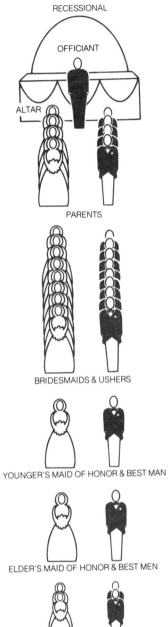

RECESSIONAL

OFFICIANT

ALTAR

PARENTS

BRIDESMAIDS & USHERS

YOUNGER'S MAID OF HONOR & BEST MAN

ELDER'S MAID OF HONOR & BEST MEN

FLOWER GIRLS & PAGES

YOUNGER BRIDE & GROOM

ELDER BRIDE & GROOM

98

Rehearsal Party Guest List

Date of Rehearsal _____

Place _____

Time _____

Phone _____

Bridal Party

Name	Phone		Name	Phone
1			16	
2			17	
3			18	
4			19	
5			20	
6			21	
7			22	
8			23	
9			24	
10			25	
11			26	
12			27	
13			28	
14			29	
15			30	

Additional Guests

Name	Phone		Name	Phone

Rehearsal Party Estimate Worksheet

	Estimate No. 1 Name _____ Phone _____		**Estimate No. 2** Name _____ Phone _____		**Estimate No. 3** Name _____ Phone _____	
	Description	**Cost**	**Description**	**Cost**	**Description**	**Cost**
Location						
Food						
Beverages						
Entertainment						
Decorations						
Misc.						
Total						

Date of Rehearsal _____   Time _____

Selected Location _____

Address _____   City _____

Phone _____   Total Cost _____

100

Your Wedding Day

Your Wedding Day

Your Wedding Day

Getting Ready

Don't be surprised if your wedding day emotions are a mixture of happiness, joyful anticipation and stage fright. This is it — the culmination of months of planning and excitement and the first day of a new life. Take it one step at a time, allow more than enough time for everything and keep calm.

Check off last minute details. Are all the transportation arrangements made? Have you specified arrival times that allow for unexpected delays and traffic jams? Reconfirm that visiting guests have rides. Some resourceful brides hire a bus or van to transport out-of-towners. Have you reserved parking spaces for bridal party cars? Check to be sure the valet parking service is scheduled correctly. Your comfort and composure come first; restrict bridal car passengers to you and your parents.

If you're dressing at the ceremony site, arrive one and a half to two hours ahead. Remember to coordinate the schedule with your photographer and videotaper.

Make notes of last minute reminders or changes for the attendants. Double check their boutonnieres and bouquets. Have the ushers secured the pew ribbons and distributed prayer books? Remind them again to be at their stations early.

Schedule time realistically. You want enough to be unhurried but not too much. A long stretch of unoccupied time is the perfect opening for butterflies in the stomach to take charge. Don't forget emergency items: tissues, extra pantyhose, safety pins, scissors, needle and thread, bobby pins, makeup, spot remover and glue. Perhaps you won't need any of them but what a comfort to know they're handy! If you get dressed at home, protect your gown by covering the car seat and floor with clean sheets.

Your groom needs a checklist as well to keep the jitters at bay. Suggest he remove all bulky pocket items for someone else to hold. Is his tie or ascot straight, his boutonniere exactly placed? Has the best man remembered the license and ring? A clothes brush should be handy for last minute grooming.

You'll feel more self-assured when you've checked every detail. Now relax and enjoy the most memorable day of your life.

Receiving Line

The reception usually starts with a receiving line. Although, when the party is small, many couples greet their guests immediately after the ceremony. It's a time to thank people for honoring your bridal day and to accept their best wishes. Some couples prefer informal visits to each reception table. But a receiving line, so rare in most social lives these days, emphasizes the distinction of the day and gives your families a chance to meet your friends.

The reception host, more often than not your mother, heads the line. After that, it's up to you who joins in and where. Our examples will give you an idea how many of them are arranged. Generally speaking, the best man, ushers and child attendants don't participate. Have each person introduce himself or herself, if necessary, and present the guest to the next in line. Long conversations should be postponed till later but you'll want to say something special to those you haven't seen recently. Take the advice of experts and remove bulky rings beforehand. Don't worry about forgetting some names. Just clasp their hands and with a friendly smile say you're too excited to remember. They'll understand.

MOTHER MOTHER-IN-LAW FATHER BRIDE GROOM MAID OF HONOR BRIDESMAIDS

MOTHER FATHER-IN-LAW BRIDE GROOM FATHER

MOTHER FATHER MOTHER-IN-LAW BRIDE GROOM MAID OF HONOR

Your Wedding Day

Reception Seating Plans

The arrangements are flexible except for one rule. The bridal couple, stars of the show, sit at the head of the table or at the most prominent one among many. We've included some examples of popular seating plans and a worksheet. The bridal table may include just parents, or attendants with (or without) spouses or dates, or a combination.

A very formal dinner almost necessitates a formal seating plan, alternating men and women. Use place cards or a seating chart adjacent to the entrance (Mary and John Doe — Table 8).

Planning the seating can be compared to creating your own recipe. Use a pinch of this, a dash of that, and stir. Seat your relatives with his and let them make their own fun swapping amusing anecdotes about your childhood escapades. Or set up a "singles" table or two and see what happens.

It's up to you. Choose a plan or let everyone find a seat. Some people think seat assignments are more orderly and encourage mixing.

Young children, in general, should be seated with their parents. Preteeners will love having a table to themselves. Divorced parents, especially remarried ones, will probably feel more comfortable at separate tables with their own parties.

Make sure your florist arranges table centerpieces that don't obstruct anyone's view. It's a shame to waste them. Plan to present them to someone special at each table: the birthday celebrant, the guest who's traveled furthest — or have the caterer put a penny under one place setting at each table.

Seating Plan Examples

GROOM'S MOTHER   GROOM'S FATHER   BRIDE   GROOM   BRIDE'S MOTHER   BRIDE'S FATHER

HEAD TABLE I

LEFT TO RIGHT — BRIDESMAID, USHER, BRIDESMAID, BEST MAN, BRIDE,
GROOM, MAID OF HONOR, USHER, BRIDESMAID, USHER.

HEAD TABLE II

FROM LEFT SIDE AROUND: RELATIVE, USHER, BEST MAN, BRIDESMAID, BRIDE, GROOM,
MAID OF HONOR, USHER, BRIDESMAID, RELATIVE, BRIDE'S MOTHER, OFFICIANT,
MOTHER-IN-LAW, BRIDE'S FATHER, OFFICIANT'S WIFE, FATHER-IN-LAW.

Seating Plan Worksheet

Toasting

Champagne is the classic beverage for toasts. But the good wishes will be just as sincere if the glass holds sparkling cider, bubbling punch, or white wine.

Usually the formal toasts begin after the receiving line and before the food is served. The best man traditionally made the first salute to the bride; today it's often to the couple. The customary toast has two parts: a reference to the toaster's relationship to the couple and a wish for their future happiness. You don't drink when you're being toasted.

The groom is usually next with thanks to his best man and a toast to you, to his parents, and to his new in-laws. Perhaps you'll want to be next with your own affectionate words for him and your parents. Other members of the wedding party can then propose any toast they wish. After the toasts, your best man can read congratulatory telegrams from distant friends and relatives.

Wedding toasts are heartfelt and usually easy to compose. If you run into writer's block, consult your local librarian for sources.

Dancing

Plan your first dance when you sense it would be right, although it's frequently before dinner. Alert your guests with a drum roll or have the master of ceremonies make the announcement that the newlyweds are about to twirl round the floor. As a rule, you dance with your father next and the groom with his mother. The best man is your next partner; the maid/matron of honor your groom's. Then it's the new in-laws turn — you with his father and he with your mother.

This order is customary but optional. In fact, if family interrelationships are very complicated, you might have your first dance and then open the floor to all. You can't expect to unravel intricate webs in one extraordinary day.

After the tensions of the day, your reception is relaxation time. By all means, have a wonderful time dancing the night away but watch out for your beautiful gown. Dancing without shoes might mean ripping your dress.

Cutting the Wedding Cake

One of the last rites of a crowded day, cutting the cake together is another reminder of your pledge to share life. Elaborate wedding cakes are often featured on their own skirted table and cut with a silver cake knife decorated for the occasion. Have your M.C. announce the event, join hands with your groom and together cut the first slice. Offer one another a nibble — it makes a great wedding album shot.

The Grand Exit

The great celebration is drawing to a close. You'll want to gather your forces for the last traditional rituals: tossing the bouquet and your blue satin garter. A dramatic stairway makes a good photogenic backdrop for these ceremonies. Decide in advance whether you or your groom will remove the garter. This is no time for any disagreement.

Say goodbye to your family and friends and exit happily through a shower of rose petals, bird seed, confetti, or time-honored rice. But check first on that. Some places discourage rice because it might damage the lawn. Let the party continue without you.

Take off for the future in your own style — a chauffered limousine, the traditionally painted and shoe-bedecked family car, or a leisurely horse-drawn carriage.

When you two look back on the day, you'll remember that your wedding had a special glow and a meaning no other day will match.

II Service Guide

Time can be the bride's best friend or her worst enemy. The luxury of six month's planning time may lull you into letting things slide until it's panic time, or you may use it productively to place your orders well in advance, allowing time for readjustments and corrections.

You and your family alone can determine how much the wedding will cost. It can range from a few dollars for a license and a civil official's fee up to many thousands. The days when families went deep into debt to marry off the daughters are gone and unlamented. Whatever you decide to spend is a personal decision based on whatever factors you consider important.

The only guideline that applies to all wedding expenditures is: use every dollar you spend to the optimum.

Shopping intelligently is a skill you learn like any other. First, you familiarize yourself with the tools of the trade and then become proficient in their use through practice. Study our shopping ABCs until you know them well. You'll be educated for bridal shopping and, in fact, for a lifetime as a consumer.

*A*sk questions. Find out exactly what services are available and their cost. Ask for references to former customers. Ask your friends for recommendations.

*B*e prepared. Know what the fashion trends are and what is in the market overall by studying magazines and window snopping.

*B*egin early. Many wedding services take time to prepare and others are in great demand. The earlier you start shopping, the more flexibility you'll have.

*B*roaden your inquiry. Don't limit yourself to the immediate neighborhood. Many companies travel widely to deliver their services.

*C*ompare services and prices. In some cases, they vary widely.

*C*ontract in writing. Be specific about details, costs, time and place. There can be no misunderstanding when it's on paper.

*C*ommunicate your budget limit and preference. It saves everyone time and makes it easier to focus on what is affordable and suitable.

*C*oncentrate on quality. It's poor economy to cut corners on excellence. Keep costs in line by eliminating extras.

And, in addition:

And, in addition:

- Remember to check hotel rooms before making final arrangements. Is there too much street noise? Will the view delight or depress you? Is there sufficient space? Ask yourself the same questions about the wedding and reception sites.
- Don't pay in full for any goods or services until they've been delivered and are to your satisfaction. You will, however, be asked to leave deposits when you place an order; in some cases, these are nonrefundable.
- If you must cancel something, check first with the local consumer protection agency to see what legal obligations you have and what restrictions a business must operate within.
- If you suspect that the information you're getting is inaccurate or that the promises are insincere, check with the Better Business Bureau to see if the company has a record of bad practices.
- It may be unnecessary to say this in the land of plastic money, but use credit cards whenever possible. Then if something does go wrong you have some clout on your side.
- When you do write checks, always make them out to the company or the individual delivering the service, never to cash.

Using Customer Savvy

Would it surprise you to know that over $20 billion are spent each year for wedding services? Yes, marriage is big business. First you spend a bundle for the ceremony and celebration. Then you start furnishing a home.

The irony of the situation is that you're buying the most when you have the least experience. It's time for a crash course in consumer savvy to arm yourself against merchants who puff up an order with unnecessary items or goldplate where sensible, everyday quality will fit the bill.

Be wary of the seller who plays on your romantic hopes in an effort to cloud your judgment. Romance is one thing, smart shopping is another. It's up to you to keep the distinction clear. Your goal when you're shopping is to make the best use of each dollar you spend by striking the best bargain.

Bargaining doesn't come any more naturally to most Americans than jogging did a few years back. But, to our credit, when we learn what's best for our health (physical or financial) we become true believers.

Service Guide

The new creed's first lesson should be: don't assume that all prices are fixed. Most items have markups, from 50 to 150 percent, that allow for some flexibility. (There are some exceptions: most department and chain stores, and some exclusive specialty shops, will not bargain.) It's standard procedure to get a discount when you order anything in large volume. If you're not sure, always start the discussion with a tentative, ''If I were to order (a large multiple) of these, would you offer a discount?'' The answer will be either yes or no. Then you'll know whether to drop the subject or go on to the next question. Some hotels, for instance, will give you a group rate for a block of rooms.

Another approach is to call a company anonymously, specify the details and ask how much one unit would cost. Once you know that figure it's simple to calculate whether the quote for a volume order includes a discount.

Be alert to other money-saving opportunities. Your florist or the member of the clergy may be aware of another wedding scheduled for the same church on the same day. The other bride might jump at the idea of sharing the cost of floral arrangements with you. Don't hesitate to suggest it.

When liquor is not included in a package deal but is being ordered for you by the caterer, consider the possibility that the price may include a hidden markup. Liquor is one of the most expensive reception costs. If union rules and state liquor licenses permit, order it yourself from a retailer. If you know a wholesaler, so much the better.

Contract Checklist

A written, detailed contract or receipt is the only way to guarantee protection for you and the merchant. Study it before you sign it and add last minute items in pen, if necessary. Start with this checklist and incorporate other services.

- Receipts for wedding gown, mothers' and attendants' dresses
- Rental agreement for formalwear
- Reception catering contract
- Florist contract
- Honeymoon travel arrangements: travel agent agreement, airline tickets, hotel reservations, visas, passports, ground travel arrangements and full itinerary
- Receipts for jewelry (also important for insurance purposes)
- Limousine service contract
- Musician agreement
- Photography and videotaping contracts
- Agreement with printer
- Reception site contract
- Bakery contract
- Bridal consultant agreement

Tipping Guidelines

Questions about tipping for services seem to cause more confusion than any others. Today the trend is toward adding a percentage to the bill for all gratuities. But it isn't done universally. Follow this guide to help you through the tipping maze.

Wedding and Reception

- **Caterer, club or banquet manager and bridal consultant**
  Reception host adds 1-20% to the bill for extra special services only. All others are covered in the fee.
- **Waiters, waitresses, bartenders and captains**
  Reception host adds 20% to the bill for servers, 2-3% for captains, or tips individuals after reception.
- **Restroom and coatroom attendants**
  Arrange with management for a flat fee or $1.00 a guest. Reception host pays at reception or with the bill.
- **Florist, photographer, baker and musicians**
  Add 1-20% to the bill for extra services only.
- **Chauffeur**
  Host usually tips chauffeur 15-20% of rental cost.
- **Civil ceremony officials**
  Usually only a flat fee of $25 and up. Some judges cannot accept money. Groom asks best man to pay after ceremony.
- **Clergymembers**
  Usually a donation depending on ceremony size. Inquire. Groom gives money to best man who pays after ceremony.
- **Ceremony assistants** (altar boy, cantor, organist, sexton)
  Sometimes covered by fee. Ask clergymember what is customary. Ceremony host pays with bill or after ceremony if convenient.

Cruising

Some cruise lines give tipping suggestions in their brochure or onboard newsletter. Otherwise, follow these recommendations: give $2.50 a day to the cabin steward and dining room waiter; roughly half for the busboy. An alternative method is also used: calculate 10 percent of the total cruise cost and divide this appropriately among the three. A token of your thanks will be appreciated by any other shipboard crew member who performs a service.

Some people disburse tips to the individual; others give the total to the purser to be distributed. The practice is to tip at the end of the trip. Unless, for example, you're lucky enough to be cruising around the world. In this case tips are given weekly.

Domestic Hotels and Resorts

In general, when in doubt about tipping, hold to the 15-20 percent rule. To be more specific, travel experts suggest 50 cents to a dollar per day for a chambermaid, left in an envelope on a bedside table or other obvious surface, and 15-20 percent of the total bill divided between the waiter and busboy. Before tipping for regular daily service ask your travel agent or the resort manager whether a service charge is added to the bill and which staff members benefit from it. For occasional room service, tip 15-20 percent for a meal, $1.00 for a bucket of ice.

Abroad

The practice of adding a service charge to the bill is nearly universal in other countries. The amount ranges from 10 to 15 percent. Even so, it's considered proper to tip 5 to 7 percent extra for special service.

Bakeries

All eyes will be focused on the wedding cake as the most dramatic symbol of your wedding celebration. It deserves to be chosen with care. Opt for a traditional cake if that's your style. Or choose something new and unusual. Either way, be sure the quality and flavor will make an impression on your guests.

Don't make the selection a chore, turn it into a taste adventure. Begin six to eight weeks ahead by calling a number of bakeries from our convenient listings. Ask what types of cakes they make and if they specialize in any flavor, style, or size. Now the important part — ask if they provide tasting samples. Many bakeries are glad to do that at no cost to you.

Then schedule appointments to taste the most tempting. And while you're there, look at sample books of available styles, sizes and decorations. You have a lot on your mind so between nibbles be sure to record prices on our worksheet. Ask for directions on the best way to cut the cake and whether they supply a cake knife.

Flavors

Yellow, white and chocolate cakes are standard with most bakeries. But you'll also find some that specialize in unusual flavors like carrot, Italian rum, chocolate fudge, mocha, or lemon. Fillings run the gamut from lemon, raspberry, pineapple, chocolate mousse, mocha and coffee to vanilla and chocolate custard, or butter cream.

Decorations

Tiered cakes are traditional and elegant. They're usually frosted white with pastel flower or border decorations. Butter cream frosting is the big favorite for a very good reason: it holds up best throughout the day. Choose the shape from circles, squares, rectangles, triangles,

or even hearts. Crown it with fresh flowers, beribbonned or in a vase, or silk flowers. The classic miniature bride and groom is still popular. Or finish it off with bells for heavenly blessings, Cupid, the Roman God of love, or love birds. Some bakeries supply festive crystal cake toppers.

How to Order

Later, at your leisure, make your choice of style and flavor. Order 6 to 8 weeks in advance. Tell the baker the number of guests you're expecting and let him suggest the appropriate size. Don't forget to ask about the "groom's cake." These are small cakes packed in individual boxes for your guests. Then relax and let the baker worry about the rest.

Save the top layer for your first anniversary celebration. Wrap it in heavy paper, tape it well, and freeze. Fruitcake keeps best wrapped in a brandy-soaked cloth and stored in a tin.

Bakery Estimate Worksheet

	Estimate No. 1 Description	Cost	Estimate No. 2 Description	Cost	Estimate No. 3 Description	Cost
Cake Flavor(s)						
Icing Flavor(s)						
Color Icing						
Shape						
Number of Tiers						
Ornaments						
Samples						
Total						

Estimate No. 1 — Name _____ Phone _____

Estimate No. 2 — Name _____ Phone _____

Estimate No. 3 — Name _____ Phone _____

Bakery Choice

Name _____

Address _____

City _____ Phone _____

Date Ordered _____

Delivery Date _____ Time _____

Total Cost _____

Deposit _____

Balance Due _____

Notes

_____

_____

Banquet Rooms and Reception Halls

Banquet Rooms and Reception Halls

Banquet Rooms and Reception Halls

For a moderate to large wedding in particular, a banquet room or reception hall can be heaven's gift to a harried bride-to-be. Here's where you'll find facilities and know-how wrapped in one neat package. In fact, many offer a package price which can include chapel, food, beverages, linens, dishes and equipment. Some provide your wedding stationery, personalized items like match covers, and flowers, wedding cake, entertainment and photographer. The fully-staffed ones supply waiters, waitresses, bartenders, parking valets and checkroom attendants. And where they don't, they'll often recommend reliable people. You have the choice of using all or some of the services, or renting the facilities for a flat fee and coordinating the services yourself.

Your first step is to phone and ask for a general description of the facilities and extent of the services. This decision is probably the most complex, knowing the shopping ABCs is a must. Make appointments with several places for complete tours. Keep in mind your clergymember's convenience if you're being married there. And bring along your worksheet to help focus on the right choice.

Discuss food and beverages in detail and ask to see samples of the tableware. In addition, make it a point to meet with members of the staff such as florist, photographer and band leader to be sure they understand exactly how you want your celebration personalized and that you understand the limitations placed on them.

These interviews are time-consuming but well worth the effort. Don't assume people sense what you want. Be specific. Companies are in business to please their customers. They do a better job of it when they know your needs.

What to Ask

You'll sense things during the tours that no amount of questioning will reveal: attitude, sincerity, adaptability and staff relations. But you'll also want to ask very practical questions. Are there adequate dressing rooms for the bridal party? Is there a rehearsal room available? Are the rooms accessible for handicapped guests?

Ask about extras like checkrooms and parking service. Are attendants available? Many rooms are so attractive that decorations are unnecessary. But, if you have something special in mind, are there restrictions? Check to see if your band will have enough electrical outlets, if they must be union members and what, if any, is the playing deadline. Is there good soundproofing between the rooms?

Room and Hall Estimate Worksheet

	Estimate No. 1		Estimate No. 2		Estimate No. 3	
	Name _____		Name _____		Name _____	
	Phone _____		Phone _____		Phone _____	
	Description	**Cost**	**Description**	**Cost**	**Description**	**Cost**
Room/Hall Rental						
Equipment: Tables, Chairs, Linens, etc.						
Food						
Beverages						
Entertainment						
A "Package": Food, Beverages, Services, Equipment, etc.						
Misc.						
Total						

Room or Hall Choice: _____

Name _____

Address _____

City _____

Phone _____

Wedding Director _____

Total Cost _____

Time To Set Up _____

Bridal Salons

Bridal Salons

*E*very bride-to-be has a fantasy of her wedding day, how exciting and wonderful it will be, and how she will look. Can't you picture it? There you are floating gracefully down the aisle — a stunning vision in white! It's true, all brides are beautiful to the onlooker. But you must *feel* beautiful to be at your best. And that means a wedding gown that's perfect for you. Don't leave it to chance. Take plenty of time and select your gown carefully.

Look at bridal fashion magazines and go to bridal fairs to get an impression of the latest look. Ask your bridal consultant to keep you posted on news of fairs and watch the newspapers. Browse through our advertisers' shops and departments for up-to-date fashions and a range of prices.

With a general idea of what you'd like and the shopping ABCs in mind, start looking with another person, probably your mother, who'll have a second more objective opinion. Don't bring more than one assistant. Choosing a wedding gown is fraught with emotion and shouldn't be complicated by conflicting opinions.

Get to know the salon expert: a salesperson, consultant or designer. They are funds of information about trends, proper fit and suitable styles. Bring appropriate undergarments and wear the correct heel height. Try to have your hair styled as you want it for the wedding to make it easier to select a complementary veil and headpiece.

Be absolutely sure before you make a final decision. Most salons require a 50% deposit when you order. Exchange and cancellation policies differ from place to place — ask to make certain. In general, it's safe to say that once an alteration has been made it will be difficult, if not impossible, to negotiate any changes. Once you have your lovely gown at home, use a wooden hanger to preserve its shape.

Bridal Salons and Department Stores

*T*hese specialty shops carry a wide selection of styles and prices, usually samples from which you order. Most of them also stock bridal accessories. They'll make necessary alterations and minor changes — different buttons perhaps or a change in sleeve style — generally at an extra cost. Be on the safe side and allow four to six months for order delays and for fittings.

Custom Salons

*I*f you crave uniqueness, a custom salon designer will create the wedding gown of your dreams. Or cleverly combine elements of ready-to-wear designs. You pay more for such personal attention, of course. Preparation time differs with individual shops but the order early caution still stands. Yet the unexpected does happen. In a pinch, a custom salon can perform miracles in a month.

Traditional Style Guidelines

*T*he pleasure of wearing something distinctive and beautiful still attracts brides to traditional wedding gowns. These are not rules but ideas of what is customarily appropriate. The important point to keep in mind is that you must feel wonderful in the dress. Keep looking around, and making notes on our worksheet, until you find the one that makes you look absolutely smashing.

Traditional Style Guidelines

CONTINUED

Fabrics change with the season. In fall and winter, crepe, taffeta, satin, moire, brocade, velvet and peau de soie are fashionable. In spring and summer, salons carry styles shaped in chiffon, lace, linen, pique, eyelet, light-weight satin and dotted swiss.

Very Formal Wedding

Gowns are floor length in formal satin, lace or peau de soie with cathedral or chapel length train. Veils are full length, headpieces are decorated with lace, beading, or silk flowers. Carry an elaborate bouquet of flowers or a flower-trimmed prayerbook. Simple shoes match the dress and long gloves complement short-sleeved or sleeveless gowns. Jewelry is optional but, if it's worn, it should be classic like a string of pearls or simple pendant.

Formal Wedding

Gowns are a little less elaborate, floor length, with chapel length or sweeping train. Wear a shoulder or fingertip length veil or a hat. With shorter sleeves, gloves are white kid, lace, or matching fabric. Carry a simple bouquet. Shoes and accessories follow the very formal style.

Semi-formal Wedding

Wear an elaborate afternoon style or simple floor length gown with or without a train. Flowers and accessories are underplayed. Veils are short with street length dresses, longer with floor length; or wear a hat or flowers in your hair.

Informal Wedding

Dresses are street length and appropriate to the season. Silk suits or jacketed dresses look good in white or any other color but black. Wear a corsage and short gloves, if any.

Choosing the Style Gown Best for You

Once you have determined the price and formality of the gown, you will want to find one to flatter your figure. Here are a few suggestions to help you select the perfect dress for your size and shape: If you're short (under five feet four inches), a high neckline with an empire waist, a short sleeved or sleeveless dress with long gloves will make you look taller. If you're tall (over five feet nine inches), a drop waist with a wide belt and trim or ruffles that wrap around the dress will take away the long-legged look. Off the shoulder, low necklines with billowy sleeves also are good. If you are of average height and weight (five five to five eight), you can get away with almost anything. You may want to select something that is appropriate to your groom's height. If you're slender, you can add a few pounds by selecting a heavier fabric such as satin, moire, or velvet. Select a blousier bodice with a gathered waist and narrow sleeves. If you're heavy, you will want to aim for a slimmer effect with a high waistline or an A-line dress with vertical lines. Stay away from lacy ruffles, clingy fabrics, and puffy sleeves. If you're large busted, a V-shape or high neckline with a keyhole yoke is usually most flattering. Avoid empire or cinched waists as they tend to accentuate larger breasts. If you have wide hips, you can disguise them with a flaired skirt or A-line dress. The wide bottom may be balanced by a broad collar, puffed sleeves, or hat.

Choosing a Train

There are three basic lengths of wedding dress trains: The Sweep, which falls about six inches on the floor and is best for semi-formal weddings; The Chapel, which falls anywhere up to twenty-two inches on the floor and is the most popular; and The Cathedral, which falls anywhere beyond twenty-two inches on the floor and is suitable only for the most formal weddings.

The four basic trains styles are: The Attached Train, which simply falls from the back end of the skirt; The Wateau Train, which falls from the back yoke; The Capelet Train, which flows from the back shoulder; and The Detachable Train, which begins at the waistline and may be removed. After the ceremony, the train should be bustled in the back to free your hands and allow you easy movement.

Bridal Salons

Choosing Veil and Headpiece

Your height, hair style and face shape affect the choice of headpiece and veil to complement your gown. If you're short, the veil should not be longer than floor or chapel length. If you're tall, hats or dramatic veiling will be striking and will not overpower you.

WREATH CAP WITH PUFFY VEIL

WIDE BRIMMED HAT

TIARA

JULIETTE CAP

Shopping for Attendants and Mothers

Before you go shopping with attendants, pick out several styles (three should be the limit) and colors that complement your gown. Leave the final choice to them. It's important that they feel comfortable and attractive too. And they will, no doubt, consider how adaptable the dress is to future use.

Bridesmaids may be similarly dressed but there's no hard and fast rule that says they must be identical. Help your maid or matron of honor choose a dress that's different enough in style and color so she stands out in your bridal party.

Shopping for Attendants and Mothers

CONTINUED

Junior bridesmaids' dresses may be identical to, or blend in with, the maids' gowns. If the style is simple and looks too stark on a young body, add adaptations like ruffles. Low-heeled, matching shoes or ballet slippers look adorable.

A flower girl wears a long or short dress that matches or complements the others. Or dress her in a white party dress sashed with fabric from the maids' gowns.

Mothers of the bride and groom usually wear full length dresses except for the most informal daytime weddings. Your mother makes her choice first then discusses colors and styles with the groom's mother. Any dressy or formal gown is appropriate as long as each complements the overall fashion scheme.

Preserving Your Gown

A wedding gown is such a powerful symbol of the happiest day in a bride's life, how to preserve it is a frequent question.

It's the rare bride who isn't nervous on her wedding day. Still, a few precautions will avoid perspiration stains. Make sure your skin is dry before donning the gown. And wear adequate shields if the style permits. Don't use an antiperspirant, it may damage the fabric.

Fabrics Differ

First, consider the fragility of the fabric before you buy. Silk, so popular for beautiful wedding gowns, is very fragile and difficult to care for, professionals cleaners say. Any stain left on the fabric starts deteriorating almost immediately. Rayon usually has sizing in it. Dry cleaning removes the sizing so that styles that depend on stiffness will wilt. Cotton, nylon, polyester, or acetate fabrics are easier to preserve.

Take Care

You'll want to relax at your reception and party along with your guests. Some staining is probably inevitable. But you can keep damage to a minimum by protecting your gown from rain and mud, lifting the train while dancing and, at an outdoor wedding, covering grassy areas with plastic.

Ask the salon attendant what cleaning method to use and whether any spot remover is safe for the fabric. Have someone rush the gown to a dry cleaning specialist within two days of the wedding. Stains become permanent very quickly. The cleaner will want to know where the stains are and what caused them.

How to Store

Many cleaners will wrap the gown in proper storage materials and some have special hermetically-sealed boxes. This will be an additional cost. Or, with care and the right materials, you can save the expense by doing it yourself. It's easy.

Never store a wedding gown in a plastic bag or on a hanger. Check the Yellow Pages for a paper company that makes acid-free tissue paper (ordinary tissue is made from wood pulp with acid in it). Cover the gown with layers of tissue, tucking extra tissue in the folds, and drape with washed, unbleached muslin. This allows it to "breathe." Line the storage area with more tissue and muslin and store as flat as possible. If you're using a wooden drawer or chest, line it first with plastic. Gowns should be placed in a cool, dry, dark place but never in a basement where dampness can occur. Air it once a year and fold in a different place to restore.

Bridal Attire Estimate Worksheet

	Estimate No. 1		Estimate No. 2		Estimate No. 3	
	Name ___		Name ___		Name ___	
	Phone ___		Phone ___		Phone ___	
	Number	Cost	Number	Cost	Number	Cost
Bridal Gown						
Veil/Headdress						
Shoes						
Undergarments						
Alterations/Fittings						
Accessories						
Total						

Bridal Salon Choice:

Name _____

Address _____

City _____ Phone _____

Hours Open _____

Salesperson _____

Color of Dress _____

Notes

_____

_____

Fabric _____

Order Date _____

Date To Be Delivered To Store _____

Date of First Fitting _____

Date of Second Fitting _____

Total Cost To You _____

_____

_____

Notes

_____   _____
_____   _____
_____   _____
_____   _____
_____   _____
_____   _____
_____   _____
_____   _____
_____   _____
_____   _____
_____   _____
_____   _____
_____   _____
_____   _____
_____   _____
_____   _____
_____   _____
_____   _____
_____   _____
_____   _____
_____   _____
_____   _____
_____   _____
_____   _____

Caterers

Caterers

Y ou want refreshments at your wedding to be top notch whether you serve choice tidbits or an elaborate banquet. Fortunately, there is such a variety of catering services you shouldn't have any trouble finding just what you want.

Generally speaking, they divide into two broad categories: companies specializing in food preparation, delivery and service only and catering departments in more comprehensive facilities.

Food specialists range from firms with long-established reputations in gourmet cuisine to new age health and vegetarian food caterers to that clever woman down the block.

Comprehensive services, like banquet halls, restaurants, or party coordinators, cater food and all, or most of, the details for any style wedding reception. Be sure you know exactly what is included. They usually employ, or have available, a staff of waiters and bartenders. And many supply furnishings, table settings and linens. Some work closely with other suppliers and will quote a package price if you ask. Before interviewing, have an idea of the reasonable cost of these services. Caterers base their price on menu, quality rental and serving costs.

What to Ask

R eview the shopping ABCs and make appointments with several caterers from our listings. Ask to taste or see samples of their food. Ask specific questions. What equipment is provided , is it part of the service, or is there a separate charge? Are labor charges additional; if so, for how many and for what services? Find out if taxes and gratuities are extra. And ask if the estimate covers table settings set-up and clean-up charges. If you're having hors d'oeuvre platters, ask how many pieces on each. Also, what brand of alcohol is supplied? As a rule, people overestimate the food to be safe. Ask who gets the leftover food, you're paying for it. Finally, when a price is quoted, note the details on the worksheet in this section.

What it Costs

B e prepared to pay a 50% deposit when you sign the contract. You want to be billed for the exact number of guests — determine the deadline for notifying the caterer. Find out when overtime goes into effect and when the balance of the bill must be paid. Postponement and cancellation policies differ. Be sure you understand the terms.

Are you thinking about doing your own catering? Then be realistic in estimating the costs. Food is one factor but you must add the cost of linen laundering, gasoline and phone bills, among others.

The catering profession attracts creative people. Give yours plenty of planning and preparation time and encourage suggestions.

Planning the Menu

M any caterers have specialties, be sure to inquire. Rather than begin with a set menu in mind, depend on the expert for advice. Check whether food will be available for guests with health or dietary concerns.

There is no "right" menu. Much depends on the hour. Wedding guests have been conditioned by tradition to expect certain refreshments at different times. A morning wedding calls for an informal breakfast or sumptuous brunch. High noon signals a seated luncheon. Wedding cake and beverage are suitable for mid-afternoon, while late afternoon suggests cocktails and canapes, or a light buffet. Early evening almost certainly means dinner; later in the evening, cocktails or dessert would be appropriate.

Stay flexible and make adjustments to keep costs within your budget. Substitute morsels of good cheese for costly smoked oysters. Or serve filet mignon but limit liquor consumption by closing the open bar earlier. When you've made your final choices, list them on our menu worksheet.

Planning Beverages

Champagne

Think of a celebration and what comes immediately to mind? Champagne, of course. Even though some people have weddings without the bubbly, they're probably in the minority. But, in fact, we use the name *champagne* indiscriminately for any sparkling white wine. It's used correctly only when referring to the wine made in the French region of Champagne. Sparkling white wines are made in other French regions and in many other countries. In recent years, American sparkling wines, called Champagne, from California and New York have gained in popularity.

Expert handling is the key to the quality of bubbling wines. The original champagne is fermented only in the bottle and costs $60 and up. Others, the bottom of the barrel, are vat-fermented. A compromise system yielding a relatively good quality wine, called "methode champenoise," ferments in one bottle and transfers to another leaving the sediment behind. Look for this designation on the label for a comparatively inexpensive wine at $8 to $10 a bottle.

An average-size bottle, 26 ounces, will yield 8 servings. For 100 guests you'll need a case of 12 to serve one drink each. That will take care of the reception toasts but nothing more. Have another case on hand for the guests who prefer to stay with champagne. Chilling is done best by packing bottles in crushed ice.

After Dinner Drinks

Following an elegant candlelight dinner, place a bottle of brandy on each table after the cake is served. Or, have waiters circulate with a cart carrying a selection of brandies and liqueurs.

Mixes

You'll want a good stock of the standard mixes: club soda, ginger ale, tonic water and bitter lemon. Also, add lime, orange and lemon juice for cocktails, and tomato juice and spices for bloody marys at a morning or early afternoon reception. Carbonated waters, like Perrier, are very much in demand these days as an alternative to alcohol.

Liquor

There's a clear trend away from dry martinis to white wine and from dark liquors, such as scotch, bourbon and blended whiskies, to vodka, gin and light rum.

Regional preferences have to be taken into consideration. For instance, bourbon is still king in the South and scotch is the drink of choice in the North and Northeast while gin is the Southwest favorite.

Thirst quenchers like vodka and gin combined with a long, cool mixer get better play in the summer; the chillier winter days call for more of the darker, richer whiskies.

You'll have to take all these factors into consideration before you place your final order. Your friends' preferences are probably familiar to you. In addition, talk to parents about what their friends like. Weigh all the elements and draw up a proportional chart similar to the one below to guide you.

If the average drink contains 1½ ounces, a quart of liquor will make 20 drinks. The average person consumes 4 or 5 drinks in an evening; those who drink wine exclusively will each use a bottle. You may have to adjust the ratio to fit your party; if you're serving wine at dinner, as an example, your total wine order may double. See our sample drink chart on the following page.

Overconsumption and Drugs

In a perfect world no wedding guest would ever embarrass you by acting in an offensive or inappropriate manner. Alas, we're only human and the potential for disruptive behavior or hurt feelings hovers over any social event where there are people with different standards of acceptable conduct.

Some people simply haven't learned how to handle alcohol, others think a wedding isn't com-

Caterers

No. of guests (based on 100)	Item	Measurement	Amount to Buy
20	Vodka	5 drinks each	5 quarts
15	Scotch	5 drinks each	4 quarts
10	Gin	5 drinks each	3 fifths
10	Bourbon	5 drinks each	3 fifths
10	Other	5 drinks each	
	Light rum		
	Blended whiskey		
	Vermouth, sweet and dry		1 fifth each
	Sherry, sweet and dry		
25	Wine	1 bottle each	2 cases white
			1 case red
10	water, soda, beer	totally generous to account for mixed liquor drinks as well	1 case club soda
			1 case seltzer
			1 case tonic
			1 case ginger ale
			1 mixed case Tab/cola
			1 case beer

plete without a rowdy scene. Do your part to control the celebration by keeping certain precautions in mind:

• Avoid salty foods such as pretzels, ham and teriyaki. They will make your guests thirstier.

• Serve high protein foods. Cheese, meat and fish help restore the blood sugar lost by drinking alcohol.

• Black coffee is not an antidote for excess alcohol consumption. All it does is wake up a sleepy drunk. Instead, it is better to drink as much water as possible, along with aspirin, to flush alcohol out of the system.

Although some people argue that marijuana and cocaine are social drugs just like alcohol, the argument doesn't hold up. Alcohol, consumed in moderation, is universally accepted as a social activity; drug use is not, in addition to which it's illegal. Drug users who confine the activity to a separate area at a large gathering, in the mistaken belief that this shows respect for the nonusers, are, in fact, seen as just plain rude by many people.

Pass the word to your friends that the drug flag is down for your wedding. It's your day and you want all your guests to feel at ease and be united in the celebration.

Hors d'oeuvres

Appetizers

Soup/Salad

Breads

Main Course

Side Dishes

Desserts

Wedding Cake

Beverages

Food & Beverage Worksheet

Food & Beverage Table Layout Worksheet

Table Ideas

* Dessert   * Cake   * Beverages
* Appetizers * Fresh Fruit (Punch,
              Display   Champagne
                        Wine, etc.)

Caterer Estimate Worksheet

	Estimate No. 1 Name _____ Phone _____			Estimate No. 2 Name _____ Phone _____			Estimate No. 3 Name _____ Phone _____		
	Number	Price Per Person	Total Cost	Number	Price Per Person	Total Cost	Number	Price Per Person	Total Cost
Food: Hors d'oeuvres, Main Course, Dessert									
Beverages: Alcoholic, Non-Alcoholic, Champagne/Wine									
Additional Services: Waiters, Bartenders, Parking Valet, etc.									
Additional Equipment: Tent, Tables, Chairs, Linens, etc.									
Complete Package: Food, Beverages, Equipment, Services, Flowers, Wedding Cake, etc.									
Misc.									
Total									

Caterer Selected:

Name _____

Address _____

City _____ Phone _____

Date To Finalize Plans _____

Arrival Time _____

Total Cost _____

Deposit _____

Balance Due _____

Notes

Consultants/Coordinators

Consultants/Coordinators

You're feeling giddy with anticipation but overwhelmed by the complex details of wedding planning. The boss is demanding overtime work and Mom is busy with her own commitments. Is there an expert to turn to who'll lift the burden from your shoulders? Yes, there is. She's the professional bridal consultant, a specialist in wedding arrangements — and, often, part-time psychologist. She'll know where to turn, how to do it and when adjustments can be made in costs without sacrificing the quality you insist on.

How Consultants Help

There are two kinds of wedding consultants: (1) independent party coordinators who will take you by the hand and assist from planning the master schedule on through to acting as M.C. at the reception and (2) company staff members who are employed by many bride-related shops and major department stores.

Typically, an independent consultant assists with the smooth flow of events whether it is wording and selecting wedding stationery or making the difficult choices in appropriate silver, china, crystal and linen. She'll help choose a fashionable wedding gown that's suitable to your style and appearance, supervise the fittings, plan the overall color scheme, advise the groom and others on proper attire and direct the reception program. She'll keep on top of schedules, expedite delivery, handle emergencies and, in general, be there when you need her.

In-house consultant services vary according to store policy and merchandise. A china shop consultant, for example, is an expert in table settings but can't be expected to advise on food. Department stores, of course, offer the greatest variety and their consultants have broad knowledge.

Independent consultants, and many in-house experts, know just where to go for the best photographers, entertainers and other wedding-related services. Don't hesitate to ask for recommendations.

Choosing the Right One

Make early appointments with consultants from our listings and come prepared with decisions on date, budget, guest list and your ideas on style. Remember your shopping ABCs. Ask whether she is experienced with the type of wedding you have in mind and what vendors she has worked with in the past. It's critical that you feel at ease with her. Brides work very closely with consultants. You'll want to feel comfortable sharing some of the subtle personal factors that affect wedding plans. Use our worksheet to keep a record of estimates and your personal reactions.

What It Costs

Staff bridal consultants are paid by their employers. Self-employed party coordinators' fees range from an agreed upon flat fee, to per guest rate, or a percentage of the total wedding costs, usually 15-20%. It's accepted practice for wedding consultants to receive commissions from the outside services they use.

Consultant/Coordinator Estimate Worksheet

	Estimate No. 1 Name _____ Phone _____		**Estimate No. 2** Name _____ Phone _____		**Estimate No. 3** Name _____ Phone _____	
	Description	**Cost**	**Description**	**Cost**	**Description**	**Cost**
Services Included:	_____	___	_____	___	_____	___
	_____	___	_____	___	_____	___
	_____	___	_____	___	_____	___
	_____	___	_____	___	_____	___
	_____	___	_____	___	_____	___
	_____	___	_____	___	_____	___
	_____	___	_____	___	_____	___
	_____	___	_____	___	_____	___
	_____	___	_____	___	_____	___
	_____	___	_____	___	_____	___
	_____	___	_____	___	_____	___
	_____	___	_____	___	_____	___
	_____	___	_____	___	_____	___
	_____	___	_____	___	_____	___
	_____	___	_____	___	_____	___
	_____	___	_____	___	_____	___
	_____	___	_____	___	_____	___
Totals	_____	___	_____	___	_____	___

Consultant Choice:

Name _____

Address _____ City _____

Phone _____

Notes _____

_____

_____

Florists

Florists

Arranging colors and varieties into exquisite floral combinations is a specialized skill. Your professional florist's advice will be invaluable in creating the mood you want and adorning your wedding setting.

Begin telephoning florists from our listings well ahead. We recommend one to three month's advance notice for an elaborate wedding. Many busy places ask for a nominal deposit to reserve their services.

Visit several to see photographs of their past wedding successes. Remember that florists are merchants who frequently have the soul of an artist. They enjoy talking about their work. So stimulate discussion by asking questions. (For example, why did you choose gladioli for this wedding? The answer will probably be that this tall, imposing flower creates a formal, traditional atmosphere). You'll get a clue to their creative thinking and take the first step to a good working relationship. Take along fabric swatches, you may decide to build a flower scheme around them. Use the worksheet for estimates and the shopping ABCs for consumer savvy.

You're in luck if the florist is familiar with the advantages and problems of your wedding and reception sites. If they're new territory, discuss the layout. It could be important to the floral design. Better yet, suggest that he or she visit them for a firsthand view.

Personal Flowers

Flowers have been a part of weddings for all recorded time—and probably before. Traditionally, the bride's bouquet has been white or pastel, with touches of color blending with the maids' ensembles. A flower-covered prayerbook is time-honored too. Less traditional but beautiful, is a bouquet of wild flowers or herbs. Have the florist blend a small honeymoon corsage into the larger cluster.

Are bouquets an absolute necessity, you ask? The answer is no. But they are certainly part of the tradition. In addition to that, they add beauty to your overall appearance and, above all, give you and your attendants a graceful place for hands.

Personal flowers should blend with your gown. They should also blend with the woman. If you're petite, it makes no sense to carry an overwhelmingly large bouquet. With the many options available, in shapes and varieties, finding the right one for your size and style is no problem. Choose from diminutive nosegays, baskets and single blooms on up to imposing sprays, cascades and long-stemmed arm arrangements.

Ask the florist to wire and wrap the bouquet. There's an unfortunate trend to the use of plastic holders which are often awkward or heavy and may drip water on your lovely gown.

Affordable bouquets or arrangements of silk flowers are gaining in popularity. You can have non-wilting, elegant replicas that rival nature's beauty. Silk-fashioned flowers are one way to avoid the shortages and high costs of out-of-season varieties. They have no preservation costs and open up your color choices to the almost unlimited hues of the dye pot.

Maids and matrons of honor occasionally carry flowers similar to the bridesmaids but, more often, theirs will be more elaborate or distinctively different. An alternative for setting your honor attendants apart is to dispense with a bouquet and have them wear flowers in their hair.

Bridesmaids carry traditional bouquets, floral wristlets, sheafs or baskets of blooms, or a single perfect rose.

Grooms today usually wear a lapel spray from the bridal bouquet and male attendants wear the customary boutonniere, often a carnation or rose.

Present your mothers with corsages to complement their gowns, or single roses to symbolize the new family union. Don't forget your grandmothers and every special person who helps.

Decorative Flowers

Beautiful sprays, stately potted palms, bowls of bright greenery — the ideas for floral decorations are almost endless. Some limits are imposed by season and availability but the sooner you order the better your chances. Consider twining entrances with blossoms, substituting flowers for an altar in a secular setting, or creating aisles with standing flower-filled urns. Many wedding cakes are topped with fresh flowers; your baker will insert a water container to hold them. Remember that churches are often dimly-lighted, a subtle color scheme may not be the best.

Contemporary Trends

One money-saving tendency nowadays is toward simpler floral decorations at the ceremony and more elaborate ornamentation at the party after.

The fashionable colors change with the seasons and styles of the moment. Your florist will know what trends are the latest.

While traditional styles are embraced by many of today's brides, they want comfort above all at the reception. The new fashion trend is to put aside the veil and headpiece and celebrate with flowers in the hair. You could use this mode to send a quiet message to your groom; each variety has a special meaning:

Apple blossoms — good fortune

Bluebell — constancy

Blue violet — faithfulness

Carnation — distinction

Forget-me-not — true love

Gardenia — joy

Lily — purity and innocence

Lilly of the valley — happiness

Myrtle — constancy in duty and affection

Olive and laurel leaves — plenty and virtue

Orange blossom — purity

Orchid — beauty

Red chrysanthemum — sharing

Rose — love

Rosemary — commitment and fidelity

White daisy — innocence

Money-saving Ideas

A profusion of flowers is apt to be very costly. Creative planning with your florist is the way to keep expenses in line. Place quality before quantity; a little greenery and strategically placed clusters of superior flowers will work wonders. Use seasonal flowers, candles, potted plants, or flowers from your own garden to cut expenses. Avoid high demand seasons — Valentine's Day and holidays like Christmas — when flowers are harder to find and more expensive.

What is the average cost of wedding flowers? Experts say to estimate 15-20% of your food and beverage budget for a guideline.

Last Minute Reminders

Be sure you include arrival time in your written contract. It should be set earlier than the photographer's arrival to allow time for setting flowers in place. Check early on your wedding day to make sure each detail is understood. You don't want any surprises as you walk down the aisle.

Florists

Preserving Your Bouquet

Whether you do your own preservation or have it professionally done, it's essential to start the process within a day or two of the wedding. Plan ahead, order two bouquets: one to throw and the other to keep.

Some florists arrange to collect your bouquet at the end of the day. But, if not, ask someone to drop it off for you.

Professionals take about three weeks to complete the process. They must first remove the moisture to preserve the shape and intensity of color. It's then sprayed with a protective solution, mounted on a satin pillow or displayed in a glass case or shadow box frame.

There are several ways to do it at home:

Air Drying
Remove all the leaves from the stem. Divide flowers into small bunches, tie stems together with rubber bands or string and hang upside down in a cool, dry place. Wait three weeks but check occasionally to be sure the string is tied tightly. When they've dried, reassemble in a bouquet and store in a covered, cardboard box away from the light.

Pressing
Some people say this is the best method for preserving the petals. Remove them carefully and lay flat on a thick layer of newspaper, taking care they don't overlap. Cover with another layer of newspaper and place a book or heavy object on top. Six weeks later mount them in a beautiful frame.

Potpourri
Remove all the petals and lay them individually on cheesecloth or window screening. When they feel like soft leather, place them on newspaper to complete drying. Mix dried petals with aromatic herbs and spices: fruit peel, mint, bay leaves, lemon balm, sweet basil and majoram are good. Add four to six drops of rose, geranium or jasmine oil from any drug or health store. Store the mixture in a glass jar for four to five months, shaking occasionally. The fragrance intensifies as it stands. Display in an attractive glass jar or put in sachet pouches.

Using an Agent
Cover the bouquet with a drying agent for at least a week or until the petals feel crisp, not brittle. Borax, cornmeal, and kitty litter, are good drying agents but the quickest, most effective, is silica gel available at most florists.

Florist Estimate Worksheet

	Estimate No. 1 Number	Unit Cost	Total Cost	Estimate No. 2 Number	Unit Cost	Total Cost	Estimate No. 3 Number	Unit Cost	Total Cost
	Name _____ Phone _____			Name _____ Phone _____			Name _____ Phone _____		
Your Bouquet									
Maid (and/or Matron) of Honor's Flowers									
Floral Headpieces									
Child Attendants' Flowers									
Hostesses' Flowers									
Mothers' Corsages (and Grandmothers')									
Men's Boutonnieres (and Grandfathers')									
Ring Bearer's Pillow									
Altar or Chuppah Flowers									
Aisle Carpet or Runner									
Aisle or Pew Decorations									
Reception Flowers									
Head Table Centerpiece									
Guest Table Centerpieces									
Cake/Buffet Table Centerpiece									
Misc.									
Total									

Florist Choice

Name _____

Address _____

Phone _____

Order Date _____

Delivery Time _____

Total Cost _____

Deposit _____

Balance Due _____

Formalwear

Formalwear

Bridal fashion magazines show the latest in men's wedding attire too. It's a good place to start. Spend a quiet evening with your fiancé leafing through their colorful pages. Later, with some preliminary ideas in mind, browse together through the shops.

Hard and fast rules for men's attire have gone the way of other wedding dictates. Today, with more colors and styles available, the choice centers on coordinating with your style and color scheme. Traditional design combinations though have stood the test of time. You'll find it helpful to have a picture of traditional styles and contemporary adaptations before you make a choice.

Traditional Style Guidelines

Formal Evening
The look is black tailcoat and matching trousers, white pique waistcoat, dressy wing-collared shirt and white bow tie. Wear white or pearl studs and cufflinks and patent or polished calf black shoes and black socks.

Formal Daytime
Gray or black cutaway jacket is worn with dark striped trousers, matching or contrasting waistcoat, white wing-collared shirt and striped ascot tie. Pearl or jeweled cufflinks and studs are appropriate.

Semi-formal Evening
Black dinner jacket and trousers are worn in winter, white in summer. A black vest or cummerbund goes with white dress shirt and black bow tie. Wear black, gold, or jeweled studs and links.

Semi-formal Daytime
Stroller jacket and dark trousers are worn with a vest, wing-collared shirt and striped or checked conventional tie. Jewelry is the same.

Informal Daytime and Evening
Wear solid black, gray or navy business suit with white dress shirt and bow or conventional tie in winter; white or off-white jacket with gray trousers, navy jacket with white flannel trousers, or white suit in summer.

Current Fashion Trends

Formal Evening
Contoured long or short jacket is worn with matching trousers, wing-collared shirt, vest or cummerbund and bow tie.

Formal Daytime
Wear a contoured long or short jacket (white in summer, dark in winter) with striped trousers, wing-collared shirt and ascot tie. A vest is optional.

Semi-formal Evening
Tuxedo jacket in a choice of colors and styles is worn with matching or contrasting trousers, white or colored dress shirt, vest or cummerbund and bow tie.

Semi-formal Daytime
Tuxedo jacket worn with matching or contrasting trousers, wing-collared shirt, vest or cummerbund and bow tie.

Male attendants and fathers can match the groom's style or contrast with a lighter or darker suit. Dress the ringbearer in a suit identical to the ushers' or any dress suit that doesn't clash. Avoid attendants' clothes that outshine the groom; and limit colors, too many might detract from the dignity of the affair.

Shopping With Your Groom

Schedule a date with your fiancé six to eight weeks before the wedding. Formalwear selections may be more limited in the busy months of April-October. The business listings will help you find convenient shops that rent or sell men's wedding clothes. In some cases, they are the same places you looked for a gown. If possible, bring along a swatch from your maids' dresses to coordinate colors. Don't forget your shopping ABCs!

You have a choice of department stores, men's clothing stores and formalwear specialty shops. If your heart is set on one hard-to-find style, consider the catalog section of some stores. It's more convenient, of course, to shop where there are many selections in stock. You'll be able to check the condition and fit of a rented garment on your first visit.

Get to know this expert salesperson too for the best advice you can get. And go prepared with your question list and estimate worksheet. How long does it take to order stock styles? Will last-minute alterations be done while you wait? What is the deadline for returns and is there a charge for late returns? Ask to see a ''damage waiver'' policy when you're renting, read it carefully and make note of the cost and extent of coverage.

Schedule fitting three to four weeks ahead (longer for someone who wears an unusual size) to allow time for alterations. Certain measurements are crucial to good fit: collars should hug the neck, shirt sleeves extend no more than half an inch beyond the jacket sleeve, jacket buttons should close easily and trousers should touch the shoetop.

When Attendants Live Elsewhere

Ask for measurement cards to send distant attendants. Most shops have them. Suggest to your friend that he be measured accurately at a shop in his city. Have the cards returned to you and note the particulars on our information worksheet. When he arrives for the wedding, his suit will be properly fitted and ready to go.

But don't take chances. Have everyone try the fit before leaving the store. And while you're there, check for missing accessories. Do all have the right shirt and tie? Are cufflinks required?

Current formalwear styles are so colorful and attractive they've become an important part of the wedding picture.

Formalwear Estimate Worksheet

	Estimate No. 1 Name Phone		Estimate No. 2 Name Phone		Estimate No. 3 Name Phone	
	Unit Cost	Total Cost	Unit Cost	Total Cost	Unit Cost	Total Cost
Groom						
Attendants						
Fathers						
Child Attendants						
Shoes						
Accessories						
Misc.						
Total						

Formalwear Shop Choice

Name _____

Address _____

City _____ Phone _____

Salesperson _____

Hours Open _____

Fitting Date _____

Pick-Up Date _____ Return Date _____

Total Cost For Groom _____

Total Cost For Each Attendant _____

Total Cost For Each Child Attendant _____

Total Cost For Fathers _____

Deposit _____ Balance Due _____

Notes

Jewelers

Jewelers

Jewelers

*E*ven with the most careful budgeting, the costs of weddings are high. By and large, you'll be paying for services that make it the unforgettable day it is. But services don't last except as memories. The one major wedding expense that endures, and appreciates in value as well, is your investment in jewelry. Your engagement ring, the wedding rings, and the fine jewelry you buy as gifts have more than symbolic value. If you and your fiancé keep this in mind (and the consumer ABCs) while you're shopping, there will be less temptation to cut corners. Depend on a reputable jeweler for advice and guidance.

Buying Guidelines

*F*ine jewelry prices are based on the quality of the metal, precious stones and workmanship. Platinum and gold are the most popular for jewelry. Platinum is the strongest metal and gold — is gold! Pure gold (24K) is too soft for rings which are made from 14K and 18K alloys.

Diamonds are a major investment. A figure equal to three weeks salary, or six percent of annual income, is recommended by experts as a guideline. Single-stone rings, called solitaires, are considered the best buy because most of the value is concentrated in that durable stone. Since diamonds are so valuable, they should be insured and policies should be updated regularly as the value increases.

The Four C's

*T*he value of precious stones is determined by four components: cut, clarity, color and carat weight. That's why a fine, small stone may cost more than an inferior, larger stone.

Cut

The cut may be round, rectangular, pear-shaped, or marquise (oval). Full-cut diamonds must follow strict standards. They have 58 facets,

The Four C's
CONTINUED

or sides, and must be faultlessly proportioned and angled to be called a "perfect" cut.

Clarity

Flawless diamonds are rare. Ninety-nine percent show "inclusions" when magnified, ranging from a tiny, white spot to a more noticeable carbon spot. These imperfections lessen the value but don't dim the brilliance.

Color

The ideal diamond is crystal clear but such stones are rare and very expensive. Most diamonds are tinged with yellow or brown. Color is considered the most important factor in price.

Carat

Stones are weighed in carats, each one divided into 100 points. The number of points determine the price, although the weight is expressed in carats for convenience. A carat, incidentally, weighs 1/142th of an ounce.

Birthstones

Diamonds have been traditional but other precious and semi-precious stones are sentimental favorites with brides. Pick your birthstone from this calendar.

☐ January — garnet or hyacinth

☐ February — amethyst

☐ March — bloodstone, aquamarine, or jasper

☐ April — diamond

☐ May — emerald

☐ June — pearl, moonstone, or agate

☐ July — ruby or onyx

☐ August — sardonyz, peridot, or carnelian

☐ September — sapphire

☐ October — opal or tourmaline

☐ November — topaz

☐ December — turquoise or lapis lazuli

Matching Ring Sets

Should you match rings or mix them? Matched sets are popular but suppose you want an heirloom ruby reset to mark your engagement, and a diamond wedding ring. No problem, just make sure the styles complement one another. Save the matching for your wedding band and his. More and more grooms are wearing wedding rings today.

How to Care for Jewelry

Soaps, lotions, chemicals in the air and skin oils leave a film on precious stones and mountings that detract from their brilliance. Make regular cleaning a part of your routine, using one of these effective ways:

Detergent

Make suds in a small bowl with mild, household detergent and warm water. Let the ring stand in the solution for a few minutes, then clean with a small brush. A clean eyebrow brush is good. Transfer to a wire tea strainer and rinse under warm, running water. Pat dry with a soft, lintless cloth.

Ammonia

Fill a container with half cold water and half ammonia and soak about 30 minutes. Use a brush to loosen dirt. Swish through the cleaning solution and drain on paper towel.

Jewelers

Commercial Cleaner

Most jewelers stock liquid cleaners especially formulated for jewelry. Usually, all it takes is a dip to clean the piece. Always avoid touching stones when you handle jewelry, hold by the end of the setting.

Machine

Small machines are available that do a quick job of cleaning any jewelry that is immersible. High frequency sound waves do the job. Each machine works differently so be sure to read the directions.

Other Care Guidelines.

• Don't wear diamonds when you're doing rough work. They're durable but can be chipped by hard blows.

• Remove rings for cleaning or laundry. Chlorine bleach may pit and discolor the mounting.

• Have a jeweler check your jewelry once a year for loose mountings, wear and for professional cleaning.

• Store your jewelry in a fabric-lined box with separate compartments. Diamonds are so hard they scratch other jewels.

• Make or buy a special jewelry travel kit. Pack a small plastic bottle of cleaner in your cosmetic case for quick touchups. Above all, don't place rings on the rim of a sink while you're washing your hands. A slight movement might send it down the drain, or you might forget it and walk away. Put it in your purse or, if nothing else is available, hold it between your teeth.

• A wrist watch should never be immersed in liquid. The best cleaning method is a jeweler's polishing cloth. Rub on the metal parts and go lightly over stones to be sure you don't loosen them.

Insurance

When you purchase your diamond, be sure to get a written guarantee and permanent registration as well as its grade and a certificate of identity. Then get a written appraisal of the replacement value for insurance purposes. List the diamond separately on your personal property insurance policy. In the event that you don't have such a policy, see about adding the diamond to your parents' policy temporarily.

Jeweler Estimate Worksheet

	Estimate No. 1 Name _____ Phone _____		Estimate No. 2 Name _____ Phone _____		Estimate No. 3 Name _____ Phone _____	
	Number	**Cost**	**Number**	**Cost**	**Number**	**Cost**
Engagement Ring(s)						
Wedding Ring(s)						
Other Jewelry: Bracelets, Necklaces, Watches, Charms, etc.						
Misc.						
Total						

Jeweler Choice

Name _____   Salesperson _____

Address _____   Delivery Date _____

City _____   Total Cost _____

Phone _____   Down Payment _____

Hours Open _____   Balance Due _____

160

Musical Entertainment

Musical Entertainment

Musical Entertainment

*M*usic is a major part of your wedding drama. Beginning with the dramatic procession down the aisle, music evokes the emotions and sets the pace until the party is over. Your choices depend, as usual, on personal preferences and budget. Do you want classical music reflecting a dignified, subdued atmosphere? Ethnic music for group dancing? Or combinations of many styles?

The ages of your guests will be a factor, of course. Suppose you're inviting everyone from greatuncle Will to teenage cousin Jane and want to please them all. Then consider alternating two musical groups at the reception.

After you've interviewed several musicians, pick two or three you like the best and ask them to arrange for you to hear them play. They may have gigs booked for public places where you could drop in.

Keep in mind that individual members within a group may change. Musicians always seem to be on the move and, what's more, the bandleader may make personnel changes to fit the music you request. Discuss the estimated cost with the leader and record them on the worksheet.

What You Should Know

*Y*ou already know the shopping ABCs. In addition, ask about versatility — how many instruments do you play? Can you play an accordian, let's say, at the ceremony and a saxophone at the reception? If you want a master of ceremonies, ask about that experience. Find out if the musicians are union members and what rules apply. How long will they play? How many breaks do they take and for how long? (Union rules mandate one 15 minute break every hour.) Will one musician continue playing while the others relax? Discuss their customary attire. Will it be suitable for your wedding theme?

All your musical arrangements should be made as far in advance as possible. Soon after you select the sites, think about positioning the musicians and/or equipment. Are there enough electrical outlets for all the equipment? Is there a shady spot outdoors? Where would they go if it rained? Last but not least, ask yourself whether a lively crowd might make floor-shake a problem.

What to Tell Musicians

*C*hoose a full orchestra, a small combo, or individuals. Discuss your plans and family traditions and customs you want to honor. A sensitive bandleader or musician will help you choose the correct music and will know what professional talent and personalities your party calls for. Almost all musicians use amplifiers. Talk about the sound level you want. Consider the timing of important announcements: when you'll make your grand entrance, dance with the groom, cut the cake and throw the bouquet.

Start with our suggestions and prepare a list of the particular numbers you want and when you want them played. Don't forget those special tunes people have requested. Go over the list early enough so your musician has the necessary instruments and rehearsal time for unfamiliar numbers. Ask for suggestions. A tight budget doesn't mean sacrificing the musical mood.

Live Music or Recorded?

*N*owadays, mobile recorded music is a popular economical alternative to live music. Complete with a disc jockey/ master of ceremonies who manages the show, mobile music productions include professional sound systems and lighting effects if you want them.

The disc jockey plays anything that comes on tape or record: classic wedding music, big band nostalgia, golden oldies and the latest rock, or new wave, disco and funk sounds. Country and western music, without doubt, are big favorites in many

regions and lively ethnic music is always in great demand. You shape your own party by requesting favorite selections when you talk it over with the producer.

Many people select mobile music because the cost is around half that of a live band. On top of that, the music can play continuously if that's the way you want it. And there's no doubt in advance about the quality of the music since, in most cases, you'll be hearing the original, best-selling recording. Space requirements are minimal — an important asset at small home weddings. A skillful disc jockey, like a band leader, will read the crowd and build a mood by selecting songs according to the response. The producer-director will also announce the highlights at the reception in coordination with the host and the photographer.

Most disc jockeys plan on taking an hour to set up the equipment.

Music Ideas

dd your favorites and list them on the worksheet.

At the Ceremony

The Wedding Song — Peter, Paul and Mary
Wagner's Bridal Chorus — Virgil Fox
Evergreen — Barbra Streisand
First Time Ever I Saw Your Face —
    Robert Flack
Three Times a Lady — Commodores
Longer — Dan Fogelberg
Mendelssohn's Wedding March — Virgil Fox
Loving You — Minnie Ripperton

For The Receiving Line

We've Only Just Begun — Carpenters
Theme from Tchaikovsky's Romeo and Juliet
You've Made Me So Very Happy — Blood,
    Sweat and Tears

Follow Me — John Denver
You Light Up My Life — Debby Boone
Beginnings — Chicago

During The Reception

Show Tunes

My Fair Lady, Doctor Zhivago, West Side
    Story, Fiddler on the Roof

Mellow Rock

I Love You Just the Way You Are — Billy Joel
Whenever I Call You Friend — Kenny Loggins
Colour My World — Chicago
Sunshine of My Life — Stevie Wonder
Lady — Kenny Rogers
When He Shines — Sheena Easton
Longer — Dan Fogelberg
We've Only Just Begun — Carpenters

Ethnic Music

Hora, polka, tango.

Ballads

Misty, Feelings, I Love You So

Musical Entertainment

Either Ceremony or Reception

Endless Love . . . . Diana Ross & Lionel Ritchie
Waiting For A Girl Like You . . . . Foreigner
Could I Have This Dance . . . . Anne Murray
Open Arms . . . . Journey
Be My Love . . . . Mario Lanza
Because of You . . . . Tony Bennett
Anniversary Waltz . . . . Al Jolson
Sunrise Sunset . . . . Fiddler on the Roof Soundtrack
Love Theme From The Godfather . . . Andy Williams
Hawaiian Wedding Song . . . . Andy Williams
A String of Pearls . . . . Glenn Miller
Feelings . . . . Morris Albert
Can't Help Falling In Love . . . . Elvis Presley
When I Fall In Love . . . . Lettermen
Just The Two Of Us . . . . Grover Washington
Always and Forever . . . . Heatwave
Annie's Song . . . . John Denver
I Love You So (aka Merry Widow Waltz) . . . .
                        McDonald & Chevalier
Unforgetable . . . . Nat King Cole
Fascination . . . . Jane Morgan
We Are Family . . . . Sister Sledge
Proud Mary . . . . Credence Clearwater Revival
In The Mood . . . . Glenn Miller
I Saw Her Standing There . . . . Beatles
Chances Are . . . . Johnny Mathis
Only You . . . . Platters
I Only Have Eyes For You . . . .
                        Flamingos or Art Garfunkle
Theme From Ice Castles . . . . Melissa Manchester
If I Didn't Care . . . . Ink Spots
Truly. Lionel Ritchie
Beautiful . . . . Gordon Lightfoot
Waiting for a Girl Like You . . . . Foreigner
Up Where We Belong . . . . Joe Cocker &
                        Jennifer Warnes
On The Wings of Love. . . . . Jeffry Osborne
You Light Up My Life. . . . . Debby Boone
More . . . . Ortolani & Oliviero
I Won't Last A Day Without You . . . Andy Williams
A Love Song . . . . Kenny Loggins
Time in a Bottle . . . . Jim Croche
Till There Was You . . . . Beatles
You Are So Beautiful to Me . . . . Joe Cocker
Beginnings . . . . Chicago

Music Selection Worksheet

Before The Ceremony

_____

_____

_____

_____

_____

_____

Recessional

_____

_____

_____

_____

_____

_____

Processional

_____

_____

_____

_____

_____

_____

Receiving Line

_____

_____

_____

_____

_____

_____

During Ceremony

_____

_____

_____

_____

_____

_____

_____

Reception

_____

_____

_____

_____

_____

_____

_____

Music Estimate Worksheet

	Live Sound	**Recorded Sound**
Name		
Number of Musicians		
Playing Time		
Cost		
Name		
Number of Musicians		
Playing Time		
Cost		
Name		
Number of Musicians		
Playing Time		
Cost		
Name		
Number of Musicians		
Playing Time		
Cost		

Music Choice

Name

Address

City   Phone

Hours Performing   Arrival Time

Total Cost

Deposit

Balance Due

Music Choice

Name

Address

City   Phone

Hours Performing   Arrival Time

Total Cost

Deposit

Balance Due

Music Estimate Worksheet

	Live Sound	**Recorded Sound**
Name		
Number of Musicians		
Playing Time		
Cost		
Name		
Number of Musicians		
Playing Time		
Cost		
Name		
Number of Musicians		
Playing Time		
Cost		
Name		
Number of Musicians		
Playing Time		
Cost		

Music Choice

Name

Address

City   Phone

Hours Performing   Arrival Time

Total Cost

Deposit

Balance Due

Music Choice

Name

Address

City   Phone

Hours Performing   Arrival Time

Total Cost

Deposit

Balance Due

Photographers/Videotape Services

Photographers/Videotape Services

Photographers/Videotape Services

Nothing will bring you more pleasure over the years than your wedding album. Begin interviewing professional photographers four to six months in advance. Most of them are in demand and that's especially true for the top-notch ones. Reserve your date as early as possible. Our listings will help you zero in on the wedding specialists. Bridal consultants can help you here. Don't take chances. Although it's possible to retake some formal shots, you'll have only one chance to capture your wedding day.

What to Look For

There's only one way to judge a photographer's work — study the portfolio. Pay attention to detail, clarity, color quality and the range of creative ideas and technical knowhow. Does the work capture the excitement and emotions of the day? Does it show skill in popular techniques: diffused lighting, soft focus, split framing, multiple exposure, among others? Discuss the specific shots you want and listen to the expert's suggestions.

Be sure you ask who shot the pictures you're examining and whether that same photographer will be shooting your wedding. Photographic skill is individual, you want to see the work of *your* photographer.

You'll be a step ahead if your photographer already knows the sites you've chosen. Ask whether other photo services are available. You might decide on photo invitations or thank-you notes. Incidentally, when you order extra prints, mention your purpose — a glossy finish, for example, is better for newspaper reproduction.

How to Order

Let the shopping ABCs and your judgment of quality, style and personal involvement guide your decision. Control costs by adjusting the quantity and sizes you

order, the album style, and the extra services. Travel costs and hours involved count as well toward the total price. Use the estimate worksheet to make informed comparisons.

Ask about a package plan, i.e., a predetermined minimum number of pictures, and compare it with a custom plan fashioned for you alone. Discounts are sometimes available when the order is larger than usual.

Your written contract should include arrival time, number of photographs, type, size and other details. It should also specify the delivery dates for prints and the cost of extras. Photographers routinely ask for a deposit when you book the date.

Study our suggestions for camera poses and give the photographer your list of not-to-be-missed shots a few weeks in advance. Quality photos take time to arrange and professionals do a better job when they're not pressured. Ideally, formal group pictures are taken, when everything and everyone is fresh, before the ceremony. But, if you're following the traditional seclusion from the groom, do it before the reception. Allow enough time to avoid rushing but not so much that you keep your guests waiting too long. Arrange for music to play and drinks to be served while they wait.

Handling Shutterbugs

There's always an amateur in the crowd who wants to capture your day on film. These shots are often more personal and great fun, so don't be discouraging. Just ask your friend to keep out of the professional's way. After all, a wedding album costs you money.

Once the honeymoon is past, take time to examine your wedding prints carefully before making the final selection. Choose a sturdy album, it will be handled many times over the years and bring you two much pleasure.

Photographers/Videotape Services

Photo Ideas

A wide range of optical effects are ideal for wedding images. Ask your expert to recommend any specialities and keep them in mind while you're looking through these ideas and adding your own.

Before the Ceremony

The bride
☐ alone

☐ dressing or adjusting veil

☐ leaving for the ceremony

☐ with officiant

☐ with parents

☐ with mother

☐ with maid of honor

☐ with bridesmaids

☐ alone at ceremony site

☐ looking out of window reflectively

☐ ready to walk down aisle

Others
☐ _____

☐ _____

☐ _____

☐ _____

☐ _____

☐ _____

☐ _____

☐ _____

The groom
☐ alone

☐ leaving for the ceremony

☐ dressing with his ushers

☐ with parents

☐ with best man

☐ with ushers

Others
☐ each one receiving flowers

☐ _____

☐ _____

☐ _____

☐ _____

At the Ceremony

☐ arriving guests

☐ processional

☐ exchanging vows

☐ presenting rings

☐ couple kissing

☐ recessional

☐ couple leaving for reception

☐ couple looking through rear car window

☐ altar and decorations

Others
☐ _____

☐ _____

Photographers/Videotape Services

Before the Reception

Couple
- ☐ together
- ☐ with bridal party
- ☐ with child attendants
- ☐ with officiant
- ☐ with guests
- ☐ bride with parents
- ☐ groom with parents
- ☐ two families together

Others
- ☐ _____
- ☐ _____
- ☐ _____

At the Reception

Couple
- ☐ together
- ☐ making grand entrance
- ☐ receiving toasts
- ☐ cutting wedding cake
- ☐ feeding cake to each other
- ☐ clasping hands (closeup)
- ☐ leaving for honeymoon
- ☐ bride tossing bouquet
- ☐ groom tossing garter
- ☐ groom carrying bride
- ☐ _____

Dancers
- ☐ couple
- ☐ bride and father
- ☐ bride and father-in-law
- ☐ groom and mother
- ☐ groom and mother-in-law
- ☐ bride's father and groom's mother
- ☐ bride's mother and groom's father
- ☐ bride's parents
- ☐ groom's parents
- ☐ bridesmaids and ushers
- ☐ guests

Others
- ☐ receiving line
- ☐ receiving line greeting guests
- ☐ food on buffet table
- ☐ wedding cake
- ☐ head table
- ☐ parent's table
- ☐ guest's tables
- ☐ musicians playing
- ☐ toasts to couple
- ☐ decorated getaway car
- ☐ guests throwing rice
- ☐ _____

Photography Estimate Worksheet

	Estimate No. 1 Name ___ Phone ___			Estimate No. 2 Name ___ Phone ___			Estimate No. 3 Name ___ Phone ___		
	Number	Unit Cost	Total Cost	Number	Unit Cost	Total Cost	Number	Unit Cost	Total Cost
Engagement Portrait									
Wedding Portrait									
Proofs									
Album									
Parents' Set									
Photographer Fee									
Misc.									
Total									

Photographer Choice

Name _____

Address _____

City _____ Phone _____

Arrival Time _____

Date Photographs Will Be Ready _____

Total Cost _____

Deposit _____

Balance Due _____

174

Photographers/Videotape Services

Videotaping, the newest fashion in wedding memories, promises to become as much of a tradition as still photographs. The equipment is lightweight and portable allowing as much flexibility and scope as you want and are willing to finance. Tape players have fast forward and rewind features for pinpointing your favorite scenes any time you're feeling nostalgic.

How to Order

Select your wedding and reception sites before interviewing companies to be aware of restrictions on videotaping activities or lighting and power problems. Some religious denominations prohibit video-taping, others allow it but restrict auxiliary lighting to maintain a dignified atmosphere. Low lighting may not rule out taping but the quality will be grainier.

Videotape wedding services are relatively new. They require careful comparisons. Look for broad experience in commercial and industrial work as well to find the seasoned professionals. Keep a record on the worksheet of the information you gather.

Preview samples of the company's past work. Ask for a description of the proposed scenario and how many cameras are necessary to do it well. Productions range from a single camera shooting from one angle to several roving ones. The best tapes tell a story rather than show unrelated clips. Although you want to rely on the professional's experience, a good producer wants to know your expectations and preferences.

Encourage the video producer and still photographer to coordinate their plans beforehand for maximum, effective use of each medium.

Two types of productions are available. One, the least expensive, uses one camera in more stationary positions. Shots are taken as the action unfolds and there's no post-production work. That means no editing, no customizing and no music although you have the option of adding these later at additional costs. The church shots, for example, are taken with one stationary camera. If a bridal party member gets in the line of sight or you and the groom have to turn your backs to the camera, that's what the completed tape will show.

More expensive productions use at least two roving cameras and remake the tape by editing. The cost increases with the complexity. An elaborate production may cost five or six times that of a simple, unedited tape.

Videotape Techniques

Directors have a variety of techniques at their command. Color tape and dual audio (microphones) are available. Your wedding music can be taped during the festivities and dubbed in later. Some tapes start with titles and a montage of 2-3 second clips. And it's possible to include interviews with friends and relatives.

What it Costs

Total cost will depend on equipment, how long the crew works, what graphics are added, and tape length, sound dubbing, photographic special effects and editing which is often the biggest cost. Equipment ranges from "home movie" video cameras to high resolution, broadcast quality cameras. Generally, companies charge an hourly rate though some set a flat fee. Decide what your wedding budget will allow and choose within those limits.

Videotaping Estimate Worksheet

	Estimate No. 1			Estimate No. 2			Estimate No. 3		
	Name			Name			Name		
	Phone			Phone			Phone		
	Number	**Unit Cost**	**Total Cost**	**Number**	**Unit Cost**	**Total Cost**	**Number**	**Unit Cost**	**Total Cost**
Videotaping Service									
Estimated Hours									
Additional Cassettes									
Editing									
Sound Dubbing									
Special Effects									
Misc.									
Total									

Videotape Service Choice

Name _____

Address _____

City _____ Phone _____

Arrival Time _____

Date Video Will Be Ready _____

Total Cost _____

Deposit _____

Balance Due _____

Notes

_____

Stationers

Stationers

Stationers

With your estimate worksheet in hand, visit a number of stationers to compare quality, services and prices.

Order all your wedding stationery at once; it's the most efficient use of your time and the best insurance for a coordinated look. Be sure to tell the stationer you want the envelopes in advance to begin the addressing and stamping. If you schedule it right, the chore will be done by the time your invitations arrive. Don't forget to order the personalized paper products you want, like napkins and matches. And consider buying pre-printed identification labels to mark each gift as it arrives with the sender's name and the date.

There's a kaleidoscopic variety of paper stocks in use today: translucent parchments, shiny metallics and plushy velours, to name three. Pastel paper colors are popular in papers and colorful inks are often used with floral or geometric border designs. Some creative couples put their photograph on the cover of an invitation, or use a custom design.

Computerization at the post office is affecting stationery orders. Because undersized, or oversized, envelopes will not go through the sorting machines the post office is charging more postage for them than for standard sizes. Wedding stationery, in particular, has always included small "informals" for thank-you notes. Now the smallest envelope one may use without paying a postage premium is 3½ inches high by 5 inches long.

How to Order

Order printing well in advance, it may take six to eight weeks. Overestimate the quantity you need to allow for mistakes, unexpected guests and for keepsakes. Set the RSVP date at least two weeks prior to the wedding, depending on how much notice your caterer needs. Plan for the ceremony to start one half-hour after the time you designate.

Consult your stationer for guidance and suggestions. Experts are invaluable at a time like this. Remember that many factors affect the price: typeface, paper stock, color and style among them. You'll find that the cost of engraving is slightly higher than printing.

An elaborate, handwritten script, called calligraphy, is becoming more popular for distinctive wedding invitations. It isn't a decision you make at the last minute — business sources say to add three weeks to printing time for the calligrapher's work. Some penmen (or women) work directly with stationers who offer calligraphy as another option along with a variety of typefaces. Other pen artists work in custom design studios where they will create and print stationery that is unmistakably yours. Prices vary widely.

How to Avoid Mistakes

Stationers are human — sometimes they make mistakes. You can take responsibility for avoiding them by asking for a proof and checking carefully before you give the final printing OK. Examine it for correct wording, line placement and spelling; check agreement of day and date, complete address and punctuation; and verify paper color and stock and lettering style. Is honour spelled with the formal "u"? Are all numerals spelled out? It's worth the trouble to be sure everything is perfect.

If you can't see a proof for some reason, ask for a replacement guarantee to avoid additional charges for corrections.

Stationery Estimate Worksheet

	Estimate No. 1 Name ___ Phone ___		Estimate No. 2 Name ___ Phone ___		Estimate No. 3 Name ___ Phone ___	
	Number	**Cost**	**Number**	**Cost**	**Number**	**Cost**
Wedding Invitations						
Response Cards/ Envelopes						
Announcement Cards						
At-Home Cards						
Thank-You Notes						
Napkins, Matchbooks, etc.						
Misc.						
Total						

Stationer Choice

Name ___

Address ___

Order Date ___

Pick-Up Date ___

Number Ordered ___

Total Price ___

Deposit ___

Balance Due ___

Transportation

Transportation

You'll feel so special on your wedding day, and look so grand, you deserve to travel in style. Chauffer-driven limousines are the traditional deluxe, travel mode and they're still very much in fashion.

How to Order a Limousine

The standard limousine, called formal, is supplied by most services. Routinely, it comes equipped with stereo and a glass divider between driver and passengers. A few firms also supply "stretch" or Rolls Royce limousines outfitted with the works — stereo, bar and color TV.

Most firms charge from the time the limousine leaves the garage until it returns. You'll probably want to rent from someone reasonably near your home. A three hour minimum rental (plus gratuity) is required by most services though a few have a two hour minimum after which they charge by the quarter hour. These standard packages are based on the assumption that mileage will be within certain limits. If you exceed that mileage, charges will be by the hour and by the mile.

Our worksheet will help you make a choice. Make your reservations at least one month in advance. Most limousine services require a deposit, 1-2 weeks ahead, ranging from 50% of the total to 100%. When there is a balance, it's expected at pickup time.

Be sure you ask about cancellation policies. If cancellation is within five days of the reservation date, some firms will return your deposit. Others reserve the right to keep all or some of it.

Limousine services schedule tightly, some over a 24-hour span. Before you place your order, be sure of pickup time and place, destinations and approximate length of rental time.

Other Travel Modes

Just about anything that moves can be used for getaway transportation — and often is! Attracted by the grace of its slower pace, many couples use a horse-drawn carriage. Antique cars and hot air balloons are favorites too. Some travel in helicopters or small, private planes. One energy-conscious pair we know peddled away on their 10-speed bikes. You're beginning a long, sentimental journey together — why not start it with flair.

Transportation Estimate Worksheet

	Estimate No. 1 Name _____ Phone _____			**Estimate No. 2** Name _____ Phone _____			**Estimate No. 3** Name _____ Phone _____		
	Style	Number	Cost	Style	Number	Cost	Style	Number	Cost
Limousine(s)									
Carriage(s)									
Classic Auto(s)									
Other									
Misc.									
Total									

Transportation Choice

Name _____

Address _____

Phone _____

Time To Be Picked Up _____

Hours Involved _____

Total Cost _____

Additional Services

We've gathered together more helpful services to make your wedding planning as easy as possible.

Quality might cost more but, in the long run, it's the best economy and certainly much easier on the nerves. Lower prices might not mean lower quality but you want to be on the alert. Ask to see equipment to be sure it's well-maintained and defect-free. Think twice about a jeweler who refers you to his appraiser. Taste food samples, specify brands, review past work.

Patronize reputable dealers. Check their references. Avoid amateurs who want to gain experience at your expense. Check with the Better Business Bureau or local consumer affairs agency if you have doubts.

Allow for mistakes. If you order well in advance and insist on early delivery dates, you'll have time to correct them.

Avoid quick decisions. Don't sign a contract until you've considered all the factors and you're sure this is what you want and can afford.

And speaking of contracts — it's essential that you get *all* details in writing: time, dates, places, deadlines and cancellation policies. You want the exact menu, the exact description of flowers, the exact itinerary. A contract is legally binding. Call the state attorney general's office if you have any questions about your legal responsibilities.

Careful planning and attention to the smallest detail are your best guarantee of a perfect, memorable wedding. The *Bride Guide* was created to help you organize and save you time looking for the services you need.

It's been our pleasure to serve you.

Additional Services Estimate Worksheet

Type of Service _____   Name _____

Address _____   City _____   Phone _____

Description _____   Cost _____

_____

_____

_____

_____

Type of Service _____   Name _____

Address _____   City _____   Phone _____

Description _____   Cost _____

_____

_____

_____

_____

Type of Service _____   Name _____

Address _____   City _____   Phone _____

Description _____   Cost _____

_____

_____

_____

_____

Notes _____

_____

Index

Index